A Georgian House on The Brink

An Early History of Peckover House;
its place in Georgian Wisbech, the Fens
and Eighteenth Century England.

By

Diane Calton Smith

Diane

15.11.16

 New Generation Publishing

Contents

Peckover House; the back steps during Flower Festival

Foreword

The House that Would be Peckover

The house standing on North Brink in Wisbech, between numbers fourteen and nineteen, is well known today as Peckover House. However, this title is a fairly recent one. When in 1948 it passed into the care of the National Trust, it was still known as Bank House, reflecting the Peckover family's long association with the banking business. It was renamed Peckover House by the Trust to honour the family who had lived there for over a hundred and fifty years.

Yet, the history of this fine house goes back much further than the Peckovers. It was built in 1722, just after the first of the Georgian kings had come to the throne and at a time when renewed interest in classical architecture was shaping towns across Britain, creating elegant new townscapes, many of which survive today.

Set slightly back from the river bank, the three storey house was designed to be lived in by the wealthy professional classes and to be run by an efficient team of servants. Despite some later Victorian additions, the main body of the house has been little changed from its original Georgian design and character, and thanks to the continuing care of the National Trust, it is still possible to imagine how some of the earliest residents would have lived and worked in it.

In August 2014, as part of my work at Peckover House, I researched and set up an exhibition called 'Peckover before the Peckovers'. The idea was to explore the early life of the house and its first inhabitants. I went on to set this information against the background of Georgian Wisbech and the Fens, and to explore the town that would have existed at that time, as well as how the social and political background of eighteenth century England would have influenced this Fenland home.

When the time came to dismantle the exhibition it seemed far too soon, especially as several visitors had asked whether the information was available to purchase. It was also clear that there remained unanswered questions, that more research was needed and that it ought to be gathered together into one book.

For Wisbech, the Georgian era was a time of prosperity and no small importance and I felt this needed to be recognised and celebrated. The research I went on to do was fascinating and in the process I spoke to many kind and interesting people who were extremely generous with their time and help. There was also a great deal of solitary reading. I gleaned information from wherever I could, but two particularly helpful sources were a book written in 1827 by William Watson, snappily entitled, 'An Historical Account of the Ancient Town and Port of Wisbech' and (thanks to Wisbech and Fenland Museum) William Elstobb's map, 'Plan of Wisbech Adjoining the River' of 1772. From these and from many other sources of information and clues, eighteenth century Wisbech emerged. Not entirely, though! There will always be a few secrets, a few mysteries, which make it all the more interesting.

So here it is then; Peckover as it was before the time of the Peckovers, a celebration of the early Georgian house on the Brink. For ease of reference, I've called the house 'Peckover' throughout. Its original name, if it ever had one, is unknown and its later title of Bank House belongs to another era, so would make no sense here. Peckover therefore seems as good a name as any. The book concentrates on the Georgian period up to 1799, as from then onwards the Peckover story has already been well told by others and it is the earlier period that needs a little time in the limelight now.

Starting with the house itself, its architecture, early history and inhabitants, the house will be set against the background of Wisbech, the Fens, then the country as a whole. Wisbech, as it was nearly three hundred years ago, gave me a few surprises, but there is also something comfortably familiar about it. As well as this, it shows the much-loved Peckover House in the earlier light of another age.

Artist's impression of the newly built house on North Brink c.1722

Chapter One

New House on the Brink

In the seventeenth century, long before the name of Peckover was known in the town, and long before the house existed that is so much a part of Wisbech today, North Brink was a cart track running by the side of the river. On one side would have been orchards and farm land, on the other the river itself, with views across open Fenland stretching almost as far as Guyhirn. Here and there, a farmhouse, barn or granary stood by the road side, but they were isolated buildings on the way out of town. Further along the Brink, away from town where Elgood's Brewery now stands, a wool comber was running his business; an indication of the importance in those days of Fenland sheep farming.

The 17th Century Reed Barn

One of the oldest surviving buildings close to the riverside, built around 1650, is the Reed Barn. It was thatched using Norfolk Reed and was constructed as a threshing barn, where farm workers would spend long, exhausting hours, flailing and winnowing wheat to extract the grain and separate it from the chaff. The thick, billowing dust that was thrown into the air during this arduous process must have created a very uncomfortable working atmosphere, but the procedure played a vital part in preparing the crop for market. The barn was positioned behind a farmhouse which, though later converted into smaller houses, remains on the Brink today. The Reed Barn became incorporated into the extended garden of Peckover House during the nineteenth century and is now in the care of the National Trust.

The early history of the land now occupied by Peckover House and its garden is far from clear. However, there are records that hint at this being the site of the hospital dedicated to St. John the Baptist, which was established in 1327 in the reign of Edward III. Pieces of stone from an ancient building were discovered in the garden and saved by Alexander Peckover, who lived here at the end of the nineteenth century and was an avid collector. Some stones were used in the garden to create rockery features, but the most easily identified is the stone used as a birdbath between the Pool Garden and Alexa's Rose Garden. This is thought to be an old church font from an ancient building on the site.

The birdbath in Peckover Garden... perhaps a font from a much older building

Information about later buildings on the site is just as hard to find, but the property deeds refer to the present house as having been 'rebuilt' around 1722, suggesting that it was not the first home to be built here. It is thought that an older house was built side-on to the river, facing a late seventeenth century Queen Anne period house across a small yard. There has been a suggestion that land along this part of the Brink, as on Nene Quay further along the river into town, was arranged into 'burgess plots', long plots that ran down to the river. This arrangement can still be seen in the 'lanes' leading to the quayside from the market place, such as in New Inn Yard. The Queen Anne house that would have faced Peckover's predecessor, across what is now the stable yard, remains today, though most of its windows have been blocked up and much of its lower floor is hidden behind later outbuildings. It now forms part of the property at number nineteen North Brink and is in the ownership of the National Trust.

The Queen Anne house that faced Peckover's predecessor sideways on to the river

7

The cellars of Peckover House are very interesting and are clearly far older than the present house. Some of the structural stone in the cellar walls is thought to be medieval and the layout of the various passages stretches to the side of the present house, much of it beneath the late eighteenth century banking wing. If the previous house did, as is believed, face sideways on to the river, the orientation and shape of these cellars would support that. Judging from the age of some of the stonework, though, the cellars most likely pre-date even the earlier house.

The cellars of Peckover House suggest the site of a much earlier building

If the early buildings on this site are hard to discover, information about the house's earlier inhabitants is even more so. Fortunately, a collection of the house's property deeds are in the care of the Wisbech and Fenland Museum and with their permission I was able to look through them. As added help, I had access to the notes written by Giles Woodgate in the 1950s, who had gone carefully through the voluminous, complicated and hard to decipher deeds. Even so, there seem to be some documents missing, so that at times a name appears as if from nowhere and then disappears again, and an exact list of owners and tenants of the house with corresponding dates is hard to produce.

The first deed available is dated 2nd August 1727 and records the sale of the house by John and Mary Stone of Brightwell, Oxfordshire for £310.10.00 to the widowed Mary Lake. The document tells us that previously John Stone had inherited the house from his brother Richard, who had inherited it from his aunt, Cicely Lowe, formerly of London. The Stone family were Lords of the Manor of nearby Walsoken Colville.

So, the first recorded owner was Cicely Lowe, who left the house to her nephew, Richard Stone, who then bequeathed it to his brother, John. The deed refers to the house as being "recently rebuilt" and this is believed to have happened about 1722, its architectural style supporting that date. However, it is not clear which of these three owners had the old house demolished and commissioned the new, much grander one.

The deeds show a pattern throughout the 1700s of the new owner of the house first becoming its tenant, and this is the case with Mrs. Lake, who is recorded as the house's occupant at the time of sale. The property she purchased was described as, "the capital messuage being lately rebuilt with the barns, stables, granaries, dovehouse, orchard and garden in Wisbech late in the tenure of John Roper and now in the tenure of Mary Lake and Thomas Lake, [quite likely her brother in law] abutting on the great river towards the south, Pickards Lane towards the north, land of Henry Gardiner towards the east and lands of John Handcock towards the west." Even at that point, the outbuildings were extensive and well equipped, perhaps remaining from the time of the older house.

Mary Lake's time of ownership seems to have been a colourful one. There are various documents indicating disputes and financial problems, including a failure on Mrs. Lake's part to carry out necessary repairs to the house. Despite the terms of the lease she'd signed with her tenants, she had neglected to keep the house in good order. As a result, a Mr. Barne, presumably her tenant, had had to spend £100 on repairs that should have been paid for by the Lakes, and the problem had to be resolved with a further legal procedure in 1733.

Mary Lake died on 12th December 1748. A few days before her death she conveyed the property to Ann Edwards, in trust for Ann Lake, the niece of Miss Edwards.

Having inherited the house, Ann didn't stay for long. She sold it to Thomas Lowry of Wisbech in 1750, who in turn sold it to William Marshall in 1751 for £550. At that time the property was described as including a brew house, wash house, laundry, barns, stable, granaries, cellars, vaults, dove house, other edifices, orchards, coal yard and garden. Mr. Marshall didn't stay long either, selling it in January 1752 to Henry Southwell of Wisbech for the same sum as he had purchased it for.

The Southwell family moved into the house on the Brink on New Year's Day 1752 and theirs was to be a forty two year long stay. Fortunately, there is far more information available on the Southwells, partly due to the roles they played in local life, but also because of the other main address they occupied in the town.

The Southwells, a wealthy family that owned a number of manors throughout England, are first recorded in connection with Wisbech in 1682, when they became tenants of Thurloe's Mansion, the property built on the site of the old Wisbech Castle. The mansion had originally

THE SOUTHWELL FAMILY TREE

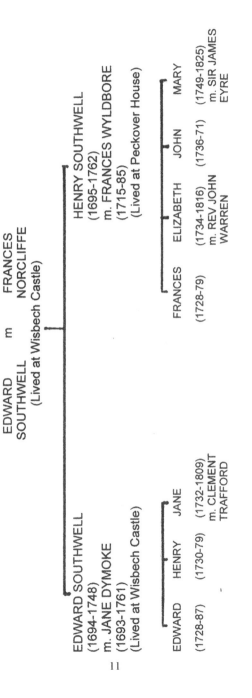

EDWARD   m   FRANCES
SOUTHWELL   NORCLIFFE
(Lived at Wisbech Castle)

EDWARD SOUTHWELL
(1694-1748)
m. JANE DYMOKE
(1693-1761)
(Lived at Wisbech Castle)

HENRY SOUTHWELL
(1695-1762)
m. FRANCES WYLDBORE
(1715-85)
(Lived at Peckover House)

EDWARD   HENRY   JANE

(1728-87)   (1730-79)   (1732-1809)
                                   m. CLEMENT
                                   TRAFFORD

FRANCES   ELIZABETH   JOHN   MARY

(1728-79)   (1734-1816)   (1736-71)   (1749-1825)
                  m. REV JOHN   m. SIR JAMES
                  WARREN   EYRE

11

been built for Rt. Hon Sir John Thurloe, Oliver Cromwell's secretary of state and spymaster. Although images of the house are rare, there is a painting of it, owned by the Bishops of Ely, in the Morning Room of Peckover House. There are also rare prints in existence, taken from an eighteenth century engraving and one of these is in the possession of the Spalding Gentlemen's Society. However, a three-dimensional view of how Thurloe's Mansion would have looked is possible by visiting Thorpe Hall in Peterborough. Thorpe Hall was built around the same time for Cromwell's Lord Chief Justice, Oliver St. John and was almost identical in design. Unfortunately, John Thurloe had very little time to enjoy his new house before the Commonwealth came to an end. With the restoration of the monarchy, the house reverted to the ownership of the Bishops of Ely. Having no need for the building, they began to let it out to local families and by 1682 the Southwells had moved in, beginning what was to be a tenancy of a hundred and five years, ending when the last Southwell died in 1787. Records show the rent in the final years to have been £30 per annum.

Henry Southwell, born in 1695, was the second son of Edward Southwell and Frances Norcliffe, who had been married on 16th January 1693 at St. Antholin's Church, Bridge Row, London. Shortly afterwards, they had moved to Wisbech and taken up residence at the Castle (Thurloe's Mansion). They had two sons, Edward and Henry. Edward married Jane Dymoke and continued to live at the Castle, taking over the tenancy from his father. Henry, who married Frances Wyldbore of Peterborough in 1725, moved with his family to a house on South Brink before purchasing Peckover House in 1752.

At that time, Henry was fifty seven, his wife thirty seven. Henry was enjoying a prominent position in the town, holding office as Town Bailiff in 1727 and 1755 and as High Sheriff of Cambridgeshire and Huntingdonshire in

1754. A Town Bailiff always held the post for just one year, but it would have been a very busy one. He would have presided over meetings of the Capital Burgesses, (see Chapter Three) and this role would have involved him at the very centre of the town's affairs. Meetings of the burgesses took place in the grammar school in Ship Lane, (present day Hill Street) so much of his work would have been local, including his duties in assisting judges at the assizes, assembling juries and collecting fines in court.

As High Sheriff, the post he held in 1754, he was the sovereign's judicial representative in the county. The word sheriff is derived from the medieval 'shire-reeve', a royal official responsible for keeping the peace. Again, the post was only held for one year. The practice of selecting the next High Sheriff was even at that time an ancient custom, having begun with Elizabeth I, and still continues. The selection is done by "pricking". A paper listing the candidates is presented to the monarch who selects a candidate by piercing the paper with a silver bodkin. Legend has it that Elizabeth I was required to carry out this selection while unable to find a pen, so used her bodkin instead.

For the first few years that Henry and Frances lived at Peckover, Henry's posts as High Sheriff in 1754 and Town Bailiff in 1755 would have kept him constantly occupied. They were both honorary posts without remuneration, the family's income being from inherited wealth from generations of land ownership. Henry was still continuing the family's tradition of buying land, acquiring the White Lion on South Brink, which at the time was called 'The Shoulder of Mutton'. His Last Will and Testament lists the property he left to his family, including a house in Meadowgate Lane in Emneth. The deed of conveyance of the Southwell property by Henry's heirs in 1794 gives a further long list of property that they had acquired. Apart from the house and garden on North Brink, there is mention of the Quaker Meeting House and part of its burial ground, some land of William Rayner and part of the estate of Dr. Wainman. Most curiously of all, the Southwells appear to have taken over the tenancy rights under old feudal law of "wine vaults sunk under the public street called the New Market in Wisbech St. Peters...near the Butter Cross containing in length one hundred and eighty feet and in breadth eighteen feet..." His tenancy rights were under old copyhold provisions, which in a continuation of medieval law, held the rights to tenancy of property from the local Manor, in this case the Manor of Wisbech Barton.

Henry Southwell, who lived at Peckover from 1752 (with kind permission of the National Trust Photo Library)

The Southwells were also very active in their own home. The house was, by the time they purchased it, around thirty years old and they may have felt that it needed updating. The new Rococo style was beginning to shape the interior decoration of fashionable homes across the country and the Southwells must have been impressed with its fluent, unrestrained mood, because they made good use of it throughout the house. The elaborately moulded plasterwork on the ceiling of the first floor landing and the intricately carved wooden frieze above the fireplace in the Drawing Room are the areas of the house where the remodelling is the most obvious.

While Henry was leading his active life on North Brink, his elder brother Edward continued to live at Thurloe's Mansion. He and his wife Jane Dymoke had three children; Edward, Henry and Jane. Only Jane married and it was to be through her married name of Trafford that the family line continued.

An intriguing glimpse into life at the mansion comes through letters written by an Italian gentleman, Guiseppe Marc Antonio Baretti during 1778 and 1779 while he was travelling. After leaving his native Italy he had travelled throughout Europe before settling in London, where he became friends with Samuel Johnson amongst others. He worked as a literary critic and writer and had already written an Italian/English dictionary before coming to England. He was known for the often scathing tone of his many letters, and the life he led was certainly very eventful. In 1769 he had been tried at the Old Bailey for murder after an incident in which he had been attacked on a London street and had defended himself with a fruit knife, inflicting a mortal wound. Samuel Johnson gave evidence as to his good character and he was acquitted on grounds of self defence.

During his time in London he visited Wisbech, staying for

two weeks with Edward Southwell at the Castle. In one of his many letters to friends, Mr. Baretti wrote, "...Wisbech I was tired of in less than the first week because my host is a man of a somewhat melancholy, rather than a cheerful disposition, and he has a mother who likes him to be in his rooms reading the Bible..."

It seems that Mr. Baretti didn't get on well with Edward Southwell. He went on to say that, although it must have been common local knowledge that there was a visitor staying at the house, no one called apart from a "fat priest" and life there, being left alone most of the time, was obviously extremely boring for this fun-loving European! Mr. Baretti also seems to have had trouble in grasping the relationship between his hosts, since Edward's mother, who was apparently encouraging all that solitary Bible reading, had by then been dead for around seventeen years! The lady Mr. Baretti referred to is more likely to have been Edward's sister, Jane. She had married Sir Clement Trafford in 1760 and they'd had two children, but the couple had marital problems very early on. It is likely that Jane, who reverted to using her maiden name, was living back at the Castle and caring for her brother by the time of Mr. Baretti's visit. She had already contested her brother's Will on the grounds of the poor man being classed as a 'lunatick'. His melancholy demeanour could therefore have been a symptom of illness, not greatly helped by his brother's death which occurred around this time.

Perhaps fortunately for everyone, Mr. Baretti's second week in the town made up for the first. It seems that he discovered the town's social scene. In sudden contrast to his down-beat description of life at Thurloe's Mansion, the tone in his letters changed to one of great enthusiasm for the social delights he discovered. His visit coincided with Race Week. This was a programme of horse races held at a course in Emneth, two and a half miles out of town. He wrote colourfully about the races and lively spectators and how, after dusk people would retire to their homes to change into more formal attire before going on to a ball held in assembly rooms in Wisbech. They danced minuets, then more energetic country dances, before sitting down to supper. This was arranged on a long table, with gentlemen seated down one side, ladies down the other. He described the good food and drink and the merry chatter, then how the expense of the meal was divided up and paid for by the gentlemen. They then went on to dance until dawn. I can't help wondering how Edward would have felt when his guest crawled in from his night on the tiles, just as everyone else was getting up!

Mr. Baretti's comments on English manners give a real insight into Wisbech society at the time. "I was much pleased with the elegant and most decorous manners of the English...without foolish flirtations, improper conversations and without altercations..." It seems we were a cultured lot even then!

On evenings when there were no races he went to the theatre. This was at a time before the purpose built theatre in Deadman's Lane opened in 1793. It seems that there were two local buildings used in the 1770s as theatres; one on the Sutton road and the other in a barn on Pickard's Lane. Could this have been the Reed Barn, now in the garden of Peckover House? It is not unlikely, since the historian William Watson says that the barn in question was later in the ownership of Jonathan Peckover. It could, however, equally refer to any other barn, perhaps long since demolished. Perhaps we'll never know! Wherever it was, Mr. Baretti was unimpressed with the theatrical scene and wrote about a "...wretched theatre, where certain poor devils of players represented some comedy or tragedy...causing perhaps still more laughter in tragedy than in comedy..."

Meanwhile on North Brink, the lively and fashionable Henry and Frances Southwell had four children, Frances, Elizabeth, John and Mary. John, their only son and Frances, their eldest daughter, never married and unfortunately there is little known of their personal lives. Only copies of Wills and a few other documents remain to provide a glimpse of them. John died very young at thirty five, leaving his estate to be divided between his three sisters, with legacies of £50 each to his aunt, cousin and the town apothecary, about whom he says, "I give fifty pounds and forgive him what he owes me." He estimated that after repayment of all his debts, his estate was worth about £4000, an enormous sum in today's values. Frances, the eldest daughter, died intestate at the age of fifty one.

Fortunately there is more recorded about the second eldest daughter, Elizabeth, who married the Reverend John Warren. He served briefly as Vicar of Wisbech St. Peters before his successful career led him to become Bishop of St. David's, then of Bangor. As a couple, they were well known as philanthropists and the extent of their good works was such that Elizabeth's younger sister Mary commissioned a monument to John and Elizabeth in Westminster Abbey. Mary herself married the wealthy and influential judge, Sir James Eyre of Wells, who was knighted in 1770.

Henry Southwell died in 1762 and left his estate, "unto my beloved wife Frances Southwell during the term of her natural life if she so continue unmarried..." Frances must have complied with this, inheriting the house on Henry's death. Then, since she outlived their only son, John, Peckover House was put into Trust on her death in 1785 for their surviving daughters, Mary and Elizabeth.

Because none of the male Southwell cousins married, the name died out on Edward's death in 1787. However, the family line continued through Jane Southwell of Wisbech

Castle and her husband Clement Trafford, and their family tree reveals some rather interesting surprises. Research has recently been carried out by Michelle Lawes at Wisbech Castle, who has been generous in sharing the information she has unearthed.

The great grandson of Jane and Clement Trafford, George Trafford Heald, married Elizabeth Gilbert, who was better known at the time under her professional name of Lola Montez, the 'Spider Dancer'. Before settling down with George, the exotic dancer had been, at various times, the mistress of King Ludwig I of Bavaria, Alexander Dumas, and the composer, Franz Liszt. Her travels across Europe and her adventures were the source of much eighteenth century gossip!

Another great grandson of Jane and Clement married into the Catholic Paston-Bedingfield family of Oxburgh Hall in Norfolk. Their descendants can be traced to the present day. In the early twentieth century Eleanor Trafford married Henry van Cutsem. Their grandson Hugh, a close friend of Prince Charles, lived at Anmer Hall on the Sandringham estate. Hugh's son William is one of Prince George of Cambridge's godparents.

In all, the Southwell family owned the house on the Brink for over forty years. Since 1785 the house had been held in Trust for Henry Southwell's two surviving daughters, Mary and Elizabeth. As was usual throughout the house's history, the property was let to tenants, the last of them being Jonathan Peckover. It appears from deeds and various other documents that he leased the house in 1794 and then purchased it in the same year for £2100. He also took over the copyhold from the Southwell estate of the wine vaults under the market place.

Jonathan Peckover, born in Fakenham in 1755, came from a family of Quakers. His ancestor, Edmund Peckover had served as a foot soldier in Cromwell's army and had become a member of the Religious Society of Friends. Although Edmund had been imprisoned for his beliefs, his religious convictions do not seem to have wavered, passing his Quaker beliefs and values down the generations to Jonathan.

In 1777 at the age of twenty two Jonathan moved to Wisbech and set up a grocery business at 25 High Street. Like many Nonconformist merchants of that time, he had not benefitted from a full education, but he made up for this through hard work and diligence. His shop thrived and he soon became known in the town for his trustworthiness. Townspeople began to ask him to hold sums of money for them in his shop safe and gradually the business began to be known as 'Peckover's Bank'. Eventually the banking side of the business took over completely from grocery and in 1792 Mr. Peckover entered into partnership with the Quaker Gurney family. Together, they formed a local branch of the Wisbech and Lincolnshire Bank. Jonathan's fortunes increased and in 1794 he leased, then purchased the house on the Brink.

His business had outgrown the shop in High Street and he set about building new premises at the side of his house. His single-storey, two roomed banking hall was set slightly forward of the building line of the house, reaching forward to the road side. His banking business was to prosper from this new site throughout his life and would continue through the generations. The historian, William Watson was in 1827 to describe Messrs. Gurney and Peckover as a most respectable firm and, judging from its success, it seems that most people agreed. The house on the Brink soon became known as Bank House, not taking on its modern title of Peckover House until 1948 when it was renamed by the National Trust in honour of the donors.

Jonathan married Susanna Payne, a fellow Quaker and they had seven children, setting up the dynasty of Quaker bankers who were to take the house and the family into the next century and then into the Victorian age.

The handsome North Brink

Chapter Two

Georgian Style on the Brink

Peckover House, set slightly back from its neighbours on the elegant North Brink, has a look that is immediately recognisable as Georgian. It is part of the handsome row of houses that greets every visitor entering Wisbech along the A47 and, like the buildings opposite on South Brink, it offers a glimpse of eighteenth century town planning. Even though several of the houses along the two Brinks have been altered and some are much older than others, it is still possible to appreciate the attempt made during the Georgian era to create harmonious streetscapes.

Built around 1722, Peckover House has a classically proportioned frontage. Its architecture follows a style that was spreading across England at the time, known as Palladianism. The style had first been popular in the early 1600s and was now enjoying a second revival. One of the earliest inspirations for it was Inigo Jones' design for the Queen's House in Greenwich, which was begun in 1615 for Anne of Denmark, Queen of James I. The Queen's House had been designed following the return of Jones from his Grand Tour across Italy, where he had become inspired by the designs of Andrea Palladio. The most fashionable architects and master builders designing grand country houses or smart town houses were greatly influenced by Giacomo Leoni's book of 1715, 'The Architecture of A. Palladio'. It quickly became the standard text book for architects and was full of illustrations of building style influenced by Classical Rome. The new house under construction on the Brink in the early 1720s was therefore right up to date and must have been quite a talking point in the town at the time.

Fashion was not the only reason for the change in

architectural style in the late seventeenth and early eighteenth centuries. There were also practical reasons for the widespread change in house design from the previously heavily timbered buildings that were part of sixteenth and seventeenth century Britain. New advances in technology, driven by the Industrial Revolution, introduced new materials and building methods. These resulted in new types of brick, plasterwork techniques, iron and glass manufacture, new paints, different lighting methods, as well as improvements in plumbing and drainage.

However, although we tend to think of building regulations as a fairly modern impact on our lives, the greatest pressure on change was the Act for the Rebuilding of the City of London of 1667, which followed the Great Fire of 1666. This Act had imposed strict regulations on all future building in order to make houses more fire-proof.

Peckover House front

The thickness of walls, which now had to be constructed of stone or brick, was fixed. The use of wood was banned from the outside of buildings, except for beams above doors or windows, and even then it had to be fire-resistant oak (later also fir). Acts followed in 1707 and 1709, adding further regulations. Compliance with these new regulations, the availability of new materials, innovation and design, all contributed to the creation of elegant townscapes throughout the country.

Externally, the main body of Peckover House is much as it would have been from its beginning in the 1720s. It is a fine example of Palladian style, which was based on symmetry and harmonious proportions. Its rows of five windows are spaced so that one side of the house is a mirror image of the other. The door is positioned in the centre, with five multi-paned windows on each of the upper floors, to give an overall square shape. This perfectly box-like appearance is enhanced by a roof that is low pitched and hidden behind a deep cornice that makes it invisible from the ground. The front door is topped by a curved pediment supported by pillars, with a fanlight above the door itself. The windows, though rectangular in proportion, have gently curved tops to them, which echo the shape of the pediment over the door. The whole building has the clean, graceful lines of Palladian architecture, which used simple mathematical ratios to determine the height of a window in relation to the width or shape of a room.

As you enter Peckover House through the front door, the Staircase Hall greets you with its simple elegance. The fanlight above the front door allows extra light into the hall. Fanlights were still a new idea, having begun to appear around 1700, but were already popular due to their being both functional and decorative. The hall runs the full depth of the house, with doors leading into all the main, original rooms. The house is two rooms deep, each lit by two windows, features typical of Palladian symmetry.

The front door with its curved pediment

All the windows in the house are of the sliding sash type, fitted with interior wooden shutters. Sash windows had gradually replaced the old tall, narrow casement type window during the previous century and were now a typical feature of house design. The popular use of multi-paned windows meant that small panes of glass could be used, which were less costly. Although plate glass had been in production since the seventeenth century and was used in mirrors, its production was labour-intensive and expensive. Shutters, which became standard by around

1700, were closed at night to provide security, as well as warmth and privacy. The shutters at Peckover are hinged in separate sections, so that only part of the window can be uncovered if required, to allow daylight in while protecting furniture from too much damaging direct light. Full window curtains were a new, fashionable addition to interior design and could be hung in a variety of ways. At Peckover they were, and still are, hung from horizontal poles.

Sliding sash windows with wooden folding shutters

Panelling with a plaster finish was still the most popular wall covering in houses and the original panelling can still be seen throughout Peckover. The plaster used at this time was based on burnt gypsum, rather than lime as earlier, mixed with animal hair or straw to aid its binding strength and durability. It was applied in two or three coats over a network of laths made of beech or oak. The walls were then painted using distemper, a traditional recipe of chalk and pigment mixed with water, and bound together with animal glue. Colours used for walls, mouldings and ceilings were pastel shades, such as light green, blue and pink. By the 1720s the shade of 'broken white', (off-white) was very popular. Paint used on interior woodwork had oil, wax or milk added to give a glossier finish. The house today is decorated in colours that are as close as possible to those used in the past, thanks to the National Trust's paint scraping research methods.

Despite the popularity of plaster, the first wallpapers were gradually making an appearance. Initially, they were imported from China and even when they started to be produced in this country, were very expensive. Although no evidence has been found of their use at Peckover, the house next door, dating from around the same period and also in the ownership of the National Trust, appears to have been papered using some of the earliest types. In 2012, when number fourteen North Brink was undergoing extensive renovation by the Trust to become a holiday let, small fragments of wallpaper were discovered. The fragments showed tiny nail holes where the paper had been tacked onto the plaster. In the days before glue had been used to attach paper to walls, it seems that it was nailed into place! The scraps of wallpaper were such a rare find that they were featured in a BBC Four documentary, 'Fabric of Britain' with Paul Martin.

A small remnant of early wallpaper showing nail holes

Cornices, chair rails and skirting boards were all used for practical purposes but were decorated with mouldings to enhance the room. Cornices covered the join between the ceiling and the wall and were usually made from plaster or wood. Chair rails, running horizontally around a room at chair-back height, were normally made of wood. Their purpose was to protect the more vulnerable plaster of the walls from the backs of chairs. Wooden skirting covered the space between the floor and the wall, protecting it from furniture and feet. The deep skirting of this period was simply decorated with a concave or ogee shaped moulding and single beading along the top. These fairly understated mouldings can be seen on Peckover's cornices and chair rails, where 'Egg and Dart' designs and rows of close-set dentils (small squares) are the most prominent.

Egg and Dart moulding

Throughout the house there is a wide range of beautifully designed fireplaces, the simpler ones used upstairs and more elaborate ones used for display in the principal rooms downstairs. The Drawing Room features a fire surround made in sections of inlaid marble, whereas the decoration used for the Morning Room features white marble that has been intricately carved. However finely modelled from the most expensive materials, the fireplaces have clean, non-fussy, classical lines that harmonise well with the rest of the house.

The Drawing Room fireplace

Even the cast iron grate at the centre of Georgian hearths had recently undergone remodelling. Around the end of the previous century it was understood that better air flow to the fire could be achieved by lifting the log basket from the floor. Before this, even in quite elaborate fireplaces, the fire had been laid directly onto the hearth, allowing no air flow beneath. Peckover's fireplaces all benefitted from the new iron baskets, to heat the rooms more efficiently.

The house most likely kept its original interior decoration for the first thirty years or so, but like any other house, changes in fashion were bound to make their mark on it. A new style, known as Rococo, had become popular in France in the 1730s. Rather than the symmetrical grace of Palladianism, Rococo design used asymmetrical lines and flowing, almost frothy shapes. Marine-based motifs, such as shells, seaweed, coral and stylised foliage, were all typical of this new wave of design, reflecting a craze at the time for grottoes decorated with shells, that were often found in the grounds of country houses. Rococo was generally thought of in England as French style and was never widely adopted here for exterior design of buildings. It did, however, appear in the interior design of a great number of fashionable houses, Peckover being one of them.

In 1752 the Southwell family bought the house and carried out work to bring the interior decoration of their new home up to date, making full use of the flair of Rococo style.

View of the landing

Leaving the front of the house unchanged, the new owners made several changes to the interior. They had the first floor landing ceiling elaborately re-plastered, decorating it with a deep cornice of curves, scallop shells, and c-scrolls with a huge central ceiling rose of flowing, feather-like swags. The Palladian window which overlooks the rear garden, and which is such a feature of the landing, is also thought to have been added at around this time.

Scallop shell detail from landing ceiling

Downstairs, one of the new features added at this time was to become one of the most talked about in the house; the carved wooden over-mantle in the Drawing Room. Topped with a huge eagle, its swags, ribbons, bows and flowers are typical Rococo.

The original door cases in the downstairs rooms were comparatively plain to start with, decorated with a modest, understated moulding. To bring them up to date, they were topped with extra mouldings and pediments. A good example can be seen above the door to the hall from the Morning Room, where the clearly plain original door case has been crowned with an extra moulding and a broken pediment.

These changes in fashion all add to the house's character and show that it was enjoyed as a family home, as well as being a show-piece for the occupants' wealth and social standing. After these mid-eighteenth century additions, however, nothing further was done to change or to spoil the character of the house, which remains very much Georgian. The family that later took possession of it in 1794 were the Peckovers. Perhaps it was their Quaker beliefs, perhaps concentration on their banking business, perhaps simply their appreciation of its eighteenth century elegance, that prevented them from greatly changing their home. Whatever their reasons, they helped to preserve the ambience of this beautiful house, cherishing it over the next century and beyond.

Chapter Three

Wisbech; Little Town on the Fen

Peckover House was built at a very good time.

Although the fact remains that this area of the Fens had its fair share of poverty, in general terms both the small town of Wisbech and England as a whole were enjoying a time of prosperity. Overseas trade was booming and the importance of Wisbech as a port was growing, with its location on the Nene and close proximity to the Wash. Many merchants had settled in the town, bringing even more business and prosperity with them, building graceful homes that exhibited their wealth and status. Peckover House was one of these beautiful new homes and was built at a time when its residents could enjoy all that life in this developing local economy could offer.

Peckover, like all large houses of the period, would have been home to two classes of people; the family and its servants. The division between rich and poor was huge, so Wisbech as a home town would have offered very different opportunities to a domestic servant with little free time, compared with those it gave to the more leisured and educated classes. Music, balls, suppers, the theatre and the races, were all available locally to people in a position to enjoy them. The poor, however, who often started work as children, had very little time, energy or opportunity to experience any of these things.

But what would the Wisbech of that time have looked like? How much of what we see today would have been recognisable back then?

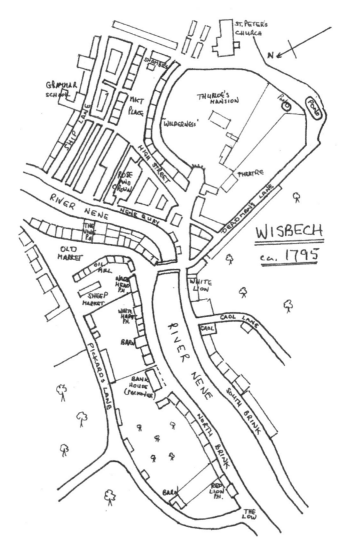

Sketch map of Wisbech c.1795

As It Was Then

Wisbech seems to have been a good town to live in. It was well run with those in authority doing their best to make improvements and to keep up with modern standards wherever possible. According to the historian William Watson, Wisbech in the eighteenth century was a "well watched" town. As far back as 1708 watchmen had been appointed, whose job it was to patrol the town at night, calling out the hour, checking that doors were safely locked, keeping a look out for fires and ensuring that drunks and vagrants were delivered to the watch constable. A police force as such did not exist at that time, the first organised force, the Bow Street Runners, not being established in London until the 1750s. Even after that, it took considerable time for provincial towns such as Wisbech to have a force of their own, so the town watch remained highly important to the town's security. The streets the watchman patrolled were mostly dark, with only meagre lighting to help him. The age of gas street lighting had not yet arrived, so any light would have been from oil lamps or candles shining in the windows of houses, or in the doorways of inns, businesses or larger homes. Candles were mostly made from tallow, which was cheap but smoked badly and smelt even worse. Wax candles were still an expensive luxury, used only by the more affluent households.

Most of the town's roads, particularly minor ones and those further away from the centre, such as North Brink, were still unpaved, surfaced only with hard packed soil. However, by 1750 the centre of High Street was paved with large cobble stones, a gutter running down the centre. Some of the footpaths were paved by then too, which meant some improvement for pedestrians, though the general state of the streets continued to be far from good. Some of the sewers running down to the river were covered over, but not all. The common sewer by the Rose and Crown on the market place was exposed to open view, only partly covered with flagstones. There were steps over the sewer to allow people to cross and this slightly elevated position was where, in the mid eighteenth century, the town crier stood to deliver his news and public notices to the assembled populace.

For fresh water, the townspeople had access to wells and a number of public pumps. William Elstobb's map of 1772 shows that there were pumps in the Old Market, Bridge Street and The Low, although there must have been several more. The Low was the area at the junction between North Brink and Pickard's Lane, (modern day Chapel Road) where once had stood a medieval cross. This cross, these days known as the White Cross of The Low, was thrown into the river, probably during the disturbances of the civil war. It was recovered during nineteenth century river dredging and saved by Alexander Peckover. Not all of the cross survived, but its remains stand today in the garden of Peckover House. The water from the pump at The Low was believed to have had medicinal qualities, especially beneficial for people with weak eyes!

The town had a weekly market and several fairs. Hemp and flax were sold at fairs on the Saturday before Palm Sunday and the Saturday before Lady Day. There were also busy horse fairs, sheep and cattle markets. William Watson goes on to mention that there was a variety of excellent shops for the sale of all kinds of articles. According to him, the tradesmen were attentive, civil and very respectable. Although he was writing at a slightly later date, he was of the opinion that this high standard had existed for a considerable time. Throughout his book he describes Wisbech as a well run and prosperous town. He was fortunate to be living in times that benefitted from the 1810 Act for Improving the Town, which brought huge improvements to Wisbech. Covered sewers, paved and neatly swept roads and gas lighting were all to come as a result of this Act. Sadly for the people living at the end of the eighteenth century, however, such benefits were still only a dream.

Mapping Out Wisbech c. 1795

In trying to reproduce the town as it was at a certain point in the eighteenth century, I settled on the year 1795 because this was an interesting time for Wisbech. Several notable buildings that would not remain for much longer were still standing, while others had just arrived. It seemed therefore a good point at which to 'freeze' time. There was no map available that matched this time. The maps I had access to were either twenty three years too early and covered only part of the area, or thirty five years too late. The missing information has been put together through research and many different sources, so the following is not a definitive picture, but should give a good idea.

Engraving of Thurloe's Mansion and St. Peter's Church (by kind permission of Spalding Gentlemen's Society)

Then, as in medieval times, the centre of the town was the market place. It occupied the same site as it does today, but behind it, where the Crescent is now, stood the grand house known as Thurloe's Mansion, which I referred to in the first chapter. This house had been built more than a century earlier on the site of the original castle for John Thurloe, Oliver Cromwell's secretary of state and spymaster. Following the Restoration of the Monarchy the Bishops of Ely had regained the house and let it to tenants for over a hundred years, the Southwell family being the most long-standing of them. With its five acres of grounds abutting the buildings of the market place and the churchyard of the medieval St. Peter's Church, the mansion would have been at the very heart of the town. The mansion, still often referred to as the Castle, was purchased at the end of the eighteenth century by Joseph Medworth, who had big ideas for redeveloping the centre of Wisbech. The town burgesses disagreed and were not in favour of his plans, a decision which was to result in Mr. Medworth demolishing his beautiful Commonwealth period home in the early years of the next century.

In 1795, however, the mansion was still standing, so ordinarily I would not go into the matter of demolition which occurred later. However, this demolition and rebuilding left us important information about the past, and at the time of writing there has been a real breakthrough in the research being done at Wisbech Castle by its Manager Michelle Lawes. Joseph Medworth was a great recycler, reusing much of the stone and features from Thurloe's Mansion in the building of his new Regency villa on the same site. Because some of these features, for example flooring and decorative moulding in the entrance hall, can be compared to those still found in Thorpe Hall, Peterborough, (Thurloe's Mansion's 'sister' house) it has long been assumed that remnants of the Commonwealth period house survive as part of the newer one.

And now there is new evidence of this recycling. When, in January 2015, I visited Michelle at the Castle, which is in fact Joseph Medworth's Regency villa, she had been stripping back layers of paint from a large fire surround thought to have originated from the older house. She had successfully exposed the underlying stone facing, which was inset with a rectangle of black marble above the fire hole, when she spotted graffiti marked with a knife in the marble.

Fairly hard to make out, but there sure enough, is written, "Trafford Esq. Born April 11 1761 at a quarter past eight at night". The date indicates the birth of Clement and Jane Trafford's first child, Sigismund Southwell Trafford, an event which took place while they were living in Thurloe's Mansion. The graffiti is proof that this fireplace once stood in the older house and was probably scrawled with a pocket knife after a night of celebration by Clement Trafford, the proud father of the new son and heir. It's good to think that although such a grand house as the mansion has been lost, there are at least some parts of it remaining and one very personal piece of history.

Fireplace in Wisbech Castle, recycled from Thurloe's Mansion (partly restored)

Fireplace in Thorpe Hall, Peterborough

But, back in 1795 the mansion, together with its stables, outhouses and gardens, was still very much a prominent feature of the town. Leaving the mansion gates behind, on the way to the town bridge was a small building called the Butter Cross, positioned roughly where the Clarkson Memorial stands today. Behind this, on the river bank, was a granary; one of many that were needed to store the huge amount of wheat produced in Fenland, ready for shipping.

As well as being a busy port, Wisbech was a market town, so the market square was where most of the town's business was conducted. The square was paved with ragstone, (thinly quarried, uneven slabs), but it appears that the surface regularly needed re-leveling and that this was done by spreading earth over the ragstone. The weekly markets must have been muddy affairs as a result, especially following a wet week. In the square itself, towards its eastern end, stood the shambles, or slaughter house and butchery, with a market cross positioned towards the opposite end. Framing the square along its four sides were a number of storehouses and commercial buildings, as well as inns and taverns, which served the many trades people, farmers, seamen and merchants who would have visited the port, the town and its market regularly. Market day was Saturday, so the town must have been crowded on that day, visitors to the market adding to the already busy quayside traffic.

Many of the hostelries around the market place have been lost, but some of their names were recorded by Arthur Oldham, a historian of the 1950s. Some of the old inns he mentioned were the Castle, the George, the Ship, (now the entrance building to the Horse Fair shopping centre) the Golden Lion, the Mermaid, the Griffin, the New Inn (previously the Black Bull) and the Old Talbot. Happily, there are also some survivors and among them the Rose and Crown is the oldest. Land tax records show that there had been a hostelry on this spot since at least 1435 and the original cellars from the earliest building form part of the more extensive cellars of today. In the seventeenth century travellers had been able to sleep in a room above where their horse was stabled, reaching their room via an open balcony (still plainly visible at the back of the hotel). Later, with the growth of the port in Georgian times the inn was remodeled to meet the more sophisticated demands of a new era. Meeting rooms, dining rooms and bars were added and a new façade was applied to the building around 1765, bringing the inn up to date with a fashionable Georgian frontage.

The inn enjoyed a thriving level of business, not just as a hostelry, but also as the main coaching inn for the town. In 1792 the London Mail Coach ran daily from here via Cambridge to the Golden Cross Inn, West Strand, Charing Cross. As well as delivering mail, the coach carried passengers and was faster than a stage coach, since it stopped only for the delivery of mail. Travelling inside the coach itself cost £1.5s.0d, but anyone hardy enough to travel on the outside of the coach, sitting at the front with the driver, could pay a reduced fare of 12s.6d. Other mail coaches ran to King's Lynn, Spalding and Boston. The same inn had also hosted since 1787 a Literary Society. Local gentlemen could borrow books, which were then expensive luxuries, from the society. It was an early private lending library for the upper classes.

17th Century rooms above stables at the Rose and Crown

In 1549, during the reign of Edward VI, Wisbech had become a corporate borough and as such had ten Capital Burgesses to conduct all necessary public business for the town. They were elected each November 1st at a meeting of the town's householders, each of whom was allowed to vote for up to ten candidates from a list. The ten candidates with the most votes took up their positions as burgesses, which they kept for one year. The ten burgesses then elected one of their number to become the Town Bailiff for that year. The Town Bailiff presided over meetings of the burgesses and acted as executive officer with overall care of the borough. (As previously mentioned, Henry Southwell of Peckover House held this position in 1727 and again in 1755.) The Capital Burgesses had no authority in the administration of justice nor in the exercise of civil power, their duty being merely to manage the estates which had been granted for public and charitable purposes and to attend to all matters arising, making sure that their actions were for the common benefit of the town's inhabitants. They could be thought of in some ways as the forerunners of modern day town councillors. Their many duties included the upkeep of local rivers, sewers, the port, the school, poor relief, and in later times, additional requirements such as town lighting. The revenue at their disposal with which to do all the necessary work came from rent from the estates they managed, profit from fairs and markets and certain other funds. The posts of all Capital Burgesses and of the Town Bailiff were unpaid. Even their annual dinner had to be paid for out of their own pocket. These were honorary positions and in the opinion of the historian William Watson, the burgesses carried out their duties unfailingly well.

King Edward's charter also served to re-establish a school in Wisbech. There had been a school in the town since the late 1300s, when the Guild of the Holy Trinity founded a free school to "educate and bring up youths". The schoolroom for this early place of learning was situated above the south porch of St. Peter's Church. However, following Henry VIII's dissolution of the monasteries, the religious guilds, along with their schools, were disbanded. King Edward's new grammar school was for the instruction of local boys in "grammatical knowledge and polite learning" and benefited from a new building in Ship Lane (now Hill Street). The burgesses were responsible for appointing the schoolmaster, who by 1790 was earning around £100 p.a. Scholarships were awarded to Wisbech-born boys, who were taught arithmetic, English, Greek and Latin for three years.

Because of the close involvement of the Capital Burgesses with the school, it seems fitting that their meetings were held in the schoolroom there for more than two hundred years. By the 1790s this was still the case.

On the western side of the square, between the market and the river, were a number of 'lanes' or yards, which facilitated the movement of goods from the quayside into the market square. Some of these, such as New Inn Yard, can still be seen today. One of the buildings in this narrow lane is a small black and white timbered medieval barn with stone flooring. Its flooring suggests that it may once have been used as stables and, although it is recorded as existing as far back as 1651, it is thought to be much older, quite possibly the oldest building in the town, apart from the church.

Black and white timbered barn in New Inn Yard

On both sides of the river at this point were a number of large warehouses and granaries, their fronts overlooking the river. Reaching up from low water level to the quayside behind the Rose and Crown was a double sided set of steps labelled as "Merchants' Stairs" on William Elstobb's map of 1772. These steps would have led passengers conveniently to the market place or straight into the Anchor hostelry, situated on the quayside close by the Rose and Crown's back door.

A considerable number of businesses were operating on and around the quayside at that time, serving the needs of shipping and the port. Among those recorded as being in business there were a blacksmith's, a chandler's and no fewer than three coffee houses.

Across the river, on the north-west side behind the warehouses, was the Old Market, the small irregular shaped centre of the Saxon settlement at Wisbech. Until the mid seventeenth century there had been a pond and a maypole there, but the pond had since been drained and by the 1790s there was a pump. Hopefully, this provided a more salubrious water supply! Around the square were houses and commercial buildings, such as a basket making business and an oil mill on the side of the square furthest from the river. The oil mill was one of seven in Wisbech by 1735, when huge amounts of flax were harvested in Fenland. The flax seed was crushed to extract linseed oil, which was then exported, the residue from the oil extraction being used as the basis for cattle feed. The 1772 map also shows both a brew house and the Vine Inn on the side of the Old Market, backing onto the river. Some very old buildings have survived, the house facing across the square towards the bridge, (now 'Granny's Cupboard Antiques'), being one of them. This building is believed to be where Jane Stuart, the illegitimate daughter of James II, had lived in earlier times. She was buried in the graveyard of the Quaker Meeting House on North Brink. (See below.)

The town bridge was the only river crossing in Wisbech and so carried a great deal of traffic. By the late eighteenth century it had been rebuilt many times, the early versions all being of wooden construction and needing regular repair and maintenance. In 1758 the first stone bridge had been built and was greeted with great enthusiasm, considered to be very handsome and a great improvement on its wooden forebears. However, there were drawbacks. The bridge was only one carriageway wide, so that vehicles often had to wait to cross. It was also steeply humped, so that carts and carriages without brakes had no way of being held back from the unfortunate horse on the rapid descent. All of this led to considerable traffic hold-ups. Some things never change!

Early 19th Century view of North Brink (with kind permission of the National Trust Photo Library)

Leading upstream from the town bridge stretched the two Brinks, the Nene flowing between them. By the 1790s, the Brinks had seen several decades of development, and were lined with barns, inns and prestigious merchants' houses, Peckover being one of them. This parade of seventeenth and eighteenth century buildings with their classical proportions and clean lines stretched out like a wide avenue with the river flowing down its centre from Peterborough and Guyhirn.

On North Brink, close to the bridge, was the old Nag's Head Inn (on the site of the later Corn Exchange), with the White Hart a few doors down. A handsome row of buildings stood alongside, including a barn and private houses, including the (modern day numbered) fourteen. This has now been restored as a National Trust holiday let, but is referred to on the 1772 map as "Mr. Wensley's". Next door to this was Peckover House, behind its handsome railings, with the Queen Anne period house (now numbered nineteen) facing sideways on to it.

On the other side of this house stood a converted pair of thatched cottages which housed the Quaker Meeting House. The Quakers, often known as 'Friends' had held their meetings here since 1711, following the Toleration Act of 1703, when persecution became less of a threat and non mainstream religions were able to speak and act more openly about their beliefs. The graveyard behind the present day building dates back to the Friends' earliest use of this site, and is where Jane Stuart was buried, as mentioned earlier.

A little further along, past a row of houses, was the Red Lion. This building, still a popular pub today, dates from 1764 and was a hostelry right from the beginning. It provided stables at the rear of the premises, so would have been well equipped to serve both customers from river craft and those arriving on horseback.

Further down North Brink, away from town, was the brewery, which by the 1790s already had a long history. One of the earliest surviving documents in the brewery's archives is a deed from 1690, showing that the property was owned by a man called Swithin Audling, a wool comber. This was at a time when the wool trade still flourished in the Fens. Fleeces were shipped from the wool comber down river to the port, by sea to Hull, then inland by canal to the mills of the Yorkshire wool towns. A later document shows that by 1739 facilities on the site included an oil mill, granaries, barns, stables, orchards, gardens and a tannery. The tannery, which treated the skins before they were shipped from the port, benefitted from its riverside location in two ways. As well as the obvious ease of transport for the finished leather, there was a constant supply of water, which was essential for the tanning process. The house at the brewery was also built at this time, predating the brewery building itself. Recent work on the house uncovered very old building methods; some of the bricks had been bonded using a mixture of mud and feathers.

Businesses such as wool combing and tanning, however, could not long survive the changes to farming brought about by Fen drainage. Acres of land that had once been good for sheep farming were now suitable for arable crops and had in some cases passed into new ownership, meaning that the traditional pastoral farming was becoming marginalised. In its place, many new crops were now flourishing, including barley, one of the main ingredients of beer! The exact date for when a brewery was established on the site is not known, but it is thought that around 1786 the oil mill was converted into a brew house. In 1795 the property was sold as a working brewery, together with four public houses. The brewery is still going strong today and has been in the ownership of the Elgood family since 1877.

South Brink was also lined with fine houses, several of which survive today. The White Lion hostelry occupied a prominent position by the bridge and was even then of considerable age, having previously been called 'The Queen's Head', then' The Shoulder of Mutton', before its final renaming in 1773 as The White Lion. As mentioned earlier, this was one of the properties owned by Henry Southwell of Peckover House. Next to it was the large residence of Charles Vavazor, the Receiver of Land Tax for Cambridgeshire. (This was the site of the future Octavia Hill's birth place.) On the opposite side of Gaol Street stood the gaol itself, or 'house of correction', as it was sometimes called. The gaol had been used since the early 1600s, when prisoners were no longer taken all the way to Ely to be tried and the legal system had become more localised.

Part of the original auditorium building can still be seen at Angles Theatre

On a more cheerful note, further back from South Brink, heading east, and close beside the walls surrounding Thurloe's Mansion, was a small theatre, which opened in 1793. The theatre reflected the new trend for touring theatrical companies and the fashionable pastime of seeing the latest play. There were a number of touring theatrical companies at the time, each with its own circuit or round of theatres they would move between, throughout the year, staying for a season before moving on to the next venue. Two such were the Fisher Theatre Circuit that owned and played at several theatres in Norfolk, and the Lincoln Circuit, whose area included Wisbech. The Lincoln Circuit owned the theatre and only opened it when they were in town. The building then remaining closed until the Circuit's schedule brought them back to Wisbech. From research using old play bills (still held in the Wisbech and Fenland Museum) it appears that the venue in Wisbech was open annually between March and May, though this most likely changed slightly from year to year. Many new plays were being written to meet the demand from provincial theatres. In addition, works by Shakespeare continued to be popular, appearing as frequently as a great many that have endured less well. A bill advertising a performance on Thursday, March 2nd 1798 shows that 'False Impressions' by Mr. Cumberland would be presented, as well as 'Harlequin's Frolicks', which was described as "an entire new pantomime."

Though the theatre building saw many changes of use and construction in the following century, part of the original building can still be seen to the side of the nineteenth century addition. Following twentieth century renovation, the auditorium is still constantly in use today, but the original layout has been greatly changed. Modern audiences now sit where the Georgian stage once was. This original stage had three trap doors, two to take a single actor and the third a 'coffin trap', which was longer in shape and useful for lifting a piece of scenery, actors or props onto the stage. The dressing rooms were situated beneath the stage. Georgian audiences were seated where the modern stage is, arranged with the pit and gallery below, and side boxes, for the highest paying theatre goers, above. From outside, the two original audience entrances can still be seen; the lower one leading to the cheaper seats in the pit and the gallery, the higher one taking the more expensive ticket holders up to the side boxes. The original venue seems simply to have been referred to as the 'Theatre, Wisbech,' but is known these days as the Angles Theatre. It is still very much part of Wisbech life, and it is hoped that, funds permitting, the original layout of the auditorium might be restored to recapture its past as one of the oldest working theatres in England.

The 1790s saw the building of a new canal. The newly engineered waterway entered town from the cast, along thc path of the modern day A1101 dual carriageway. It replaced the ancient and overgrown Well Stream, which for centuries had meandered on its sluggish journey from Outwell. Successive changes to the rivers had long since rendered the Well Stream unnavigable and throughout the 1700s plans for a new canal to be cut in a direct line from Outwell, had been discussed. In 1792 a meeting was held for local people and potential share-holders to get the project off the ground. By 1796 the new canal was opened between Outwell and Wisbech, joining the Nene near the modern-day Freedom Bridge. By re-establishing the old link with the Ouse, Wisbech was now connected by water with Cambridge and Huntingdon, as well as with Norfolk and Suffolk.

The eighteenth century had introduced workhouses to most towns in an attempt to alleviate the desperate need that many people were suffering. Workhouses have never enjoyed a good reputation, but it seems that the one in Wisbech was better run than most. It was situated close to the Horse Fair, behind the market square and had been built in 1722 by the Capital Burgesses. It could hold up to eighty residents, with separate relief for others in need, who did not live in the workhouse itself. The cost to the borough was recorded as three shillings per head per week by the end of the 1700s and according to the historian, William Watson, it was "neat and respectable".

Georgian Wisbech, despite its muddy streets and less than ideal sanitation, was a well run, prosperous port and market town. With its administration and development, its trade and culture, it would have been a place of colour, innovation and bustle. The next century was to bring further development and improved transport systems, but the Georgian age brought elegance, efficiency and prosperity, forming a solid basis for future Victorian enterprise.

Fenland is perhaps one of England's least celebrated landscapes

Chapter Four

The Fen and its Tigers

The town of Wisbech rises from the wide swathe of Fenland in the East of England, and is in truth inseparable from it. Travelling towards the town from any direction tells you that. The seemingly endless, open, sometimes bleak vastness stretches towards a distant horizon that is often devoid of trees or buildings. Its dark soil, yielding crops season after season, its huge panoramic skies, so often painted and photographed, are as well known as its down-sides; its perceived lack of glamour and its back-water image.

The Fen is ancient. Constantly changing, while keeping its traditions close and often guarded, Fenland is home to its old towns; to Whittlesey, March, Ely, Ramsey and Wisbech, to name but a few. These towns are as aged as the Fen itself, stirring to life as settlements long before history recorded them, and they have always been reliant on the land around them. In good times and in bad, the town and the Fen looked to each other, and important to them both was the network of waterways that ran through them, nourishing them. For drainage, transport, lifeblood, it would be impossible to understand Wisbech or any of the other Fenland towns without looking at the significance of the Fen itself and its rivers.

Practically the first thing that anyone notices as they enter Wisbech from the Peterborough direction is the river that curves through it, dominating the town as it goes. Seeing that great body of water now, it is hard to imagine what a complicated and difficult history it has had and how often its course has been changed. Each reshaping has had a huge effect on the people living by it and each change has made its impact felt for centuries.

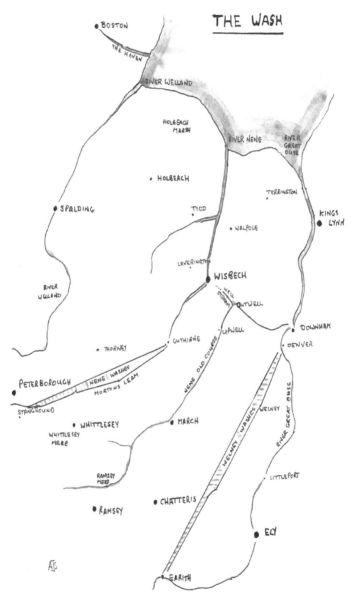

THE WASH

BOSTON

THE HAVEN

RIVER WELLAND

HOLBEACH MARSH

RIVER NENE

RIVER GREAT OUSE

HOLBEACH

TERRINGTON

SPALDING

TYDD

KINGS LYNN

WALPOLE

LEVERINGTON

WISBECH

RIVER WELLAND

NEW STREAM

OUTWELL

UPWELL

DOWNHAM

THORNEY

GUYHIRNE

DENVER

PETERBOROUGH

NENE WASHES

MORTONS LEAM

NENE OLD COURSE

STANGROUND

WHITTLESEY

WHITTLESEY MERE

MARCH

WELNEY WASHES

WELNEY

RIVER GREAT OUSE

RAMSEY MERE

LITTLEPORT

CHATTERIS

RAMSEY

ELY

AJS

EARITH

Sketch Map of the towns and villages of Fenland

54

The Meandering Tale of the Nene

Going right back to the time when the sea came further inland, the then much larger Wash had a line of villages growing up around it on the silt Fen; Terrington, Walpole, Wisbech, Leverington, Tydd and Holbeach. Further inland other villages, such as March and Ely evolved on islands of clay between areas of water-logged peat fen.

By the post-Roman era the River Ouse still entered the Wash at Wisbech, having flowed through Outwell from Littleport. As for the River Nene, it had two main branches, the northern one entering the Wash near modern day Tydd, with the southern branch running via the island of March and linking with the Ouse at Outwell, the two rivers sharing an outfall via the Well Stream at Wisbech.

The earliest settlement at Wisbech is thought to have been roughly where the modern day Old Market is situated, and would have been no more than a tiny hamlet of wildfowlers. There are quite a few suggestions for the origin of the town's name, but one of the more likely seems to be 'Ouse Beach', because its early prosperity was linked to its proximity to the sea. William the Conqueror selected this tiny place close to the Wash, with its connections to the interior via a system of waterways, to build a castle. He relied upon supplies being shipped in from Normandy, and Wisbech with its position between the Wash and the Fens became a place of strategic importance. Wisbech Castle became the administrative centre for the area, its position perfect for overseeing the surrounding Fens and waterways. The Bishops of Ely, whose responsibilities included overall control of the Fen, its produce and all water borne commercial trade from the Wash into the rivers, ran the area's administration from the castle.

The Fens were already recognised for their abundance of eels and water fowl. The Domesday survey of 1080 recorded that revenue from eel catching was already significant by that time. To make the most of this abundance, the Bishops set up a number of fisheries in the Fenland manors that they established during the next few decades. Fish and eels were a highly important part of the medieval diet, with eels even used in some circumstances as payment for rent.

The town that grew up around Wisbech Castle quickly increased in size and importance, its market and port with it. The townspeople gradually moved from their old settlement on the north western river bank to a new position close by the protection of the castle walls. The new market place established at that time has remained ever since and is still used today.

The Well Stream continued to provide a link between the two rivers and the sea, being used increasingly over the centuries for the transport of goods and people. A healthy trade had developed, exporting wool, lamb, sedge and other Fen produce and the villages of Upwell and Outwell soon became prosperous as a result. However, the Wash was gradually silting up and the outflow of the Well Stream at Wisbech was becoming more and more difficult to navigate. By the thirteenth century, it had become obvious to the Bishop of Ely that somewhere other than Wisbech would have to be used to provide an outfall for the Ouse. In 1250 the necessary work was carried out, diverting the Ouse to a new exit to the Wash at King's Lynn. A channel was cut from Littleport to Denver, linking with the rivers at Lynn.

However beneficial this must have been for trade through the port of King's Lynn, it had the opposite effect on Wisbech. River traffic heading for the Wash no longer passed through the town and the waterways serving it continued to deteriorate rapidly.

To make problems worse, the Nene further upstream was also suffering from the build-up of silt. In those days, the section of the Nene between Peterborough and Guyhirn consisted of a meandering system of forks and inland lakes called meres. Continuous deterioration of these waterways meant they were navigable for only part of the year.

Around the middle of the fifteenth century a later Bishop of Ely, Bishop Morton, realised that significant action was necessary. Rather than just dredging the existing rivers, he decided that the only lasting way forward was to create a completely new, straight cut. He instigated the cutting of a twelve mile long, straight channel from Stanground to Guyhirn, which became known as Morton's Leam. At Guyhirn the new cut joined a local channel running to Wisbech, thus creating a direct waterway from Peterborough to Wisbech. It was a huge improvement, and of great significance for Wisbech's long-suffering river trade. According to records of the time, the sudden benefits from Morton's Leam were so great, and the flow of water so improved, that the volume of water could hardly pass under Wisbech town bridge!

This change without doubt improved the lot of Wisbech for a good period of time, but no improvements, however well done, could last forever. There was a constant threat from the natural silting-up of the Wash and the rivers, and in time navigation once more became difficult. Lighters, the flat bottomed barges used along Fen rivers to carry cargo to and from larger boats, often became stranded on the mud at low tide. Cargoes were frequently delayed and even worse, in a few cases goods were stolen, a situation that was totally unacceptable to ship owners and merchants.

The monasteries during the medieval period, and later the

bishops, had carried out continual maintenance of the waterways and the Fen, but after 1538 when Henry VIII effected his infamous dissolution of the monasteries, all this work came to an abrupt end. By the seventeenth century the situation had deteriorated so badly that much more than simple maintenance was necessary. Radical change was required.

This came with Vermuyden's huge operation in two phases to drain the Fens. This work was widespread and benefitted navigation as well as drainage. As part of this work, in 1651 a new cut was made from Peterborough to Guyhirn, running parallel to Morton's Leam. The land between the two channels, used for grazing in summer and as a holding ground for flood water in winter, was known as the Nene Washes. The resulting route, together with the earlier established straight cut from Guyhirn to Wisbech, gave the Nene the form it has today.

In 1663 the Bedford Level Corporation was formed to do the work that the monasteries had carried out before the dissolution. They became responsible for the upkeep of drains, banks, sluices, bridges and the needs of navigation. The corporation tried to fund their work through taxation of the newly drained land, but the costs of drainage had been so high that there was never enough money to do the necessary work and maintenance began to be neglected.

Added to this, drainage itself created problems. When the peat Fen soil dried out, it shrank and throughout the late 1600s it was becoming increasingly obvious that this was a widespread problem. Huge areas of peat Fen were shrinking to such an extent that they were soon at a lower level than the waterways they were meant to be draining into. The peat areas were also lower than the silt Fen at the edge of the Wash, through which rivers had to flow to reach the sea. Something was needed to lift volumes of water from a lower level to a higher one, rather than merely to rely on drainage and gravity, a situation that was no longer practical. Windmills were gradually introduced to do just that.

Constructed at any point across Fenland where water needed to be lifted from a lower level to a higher one, such as from a minor drainage dyke into a river, these new windmills must have made quite an impact on the landscape. When Daniel Defoe travelled around Britain in 1724-27 the Cambridgeshire and Lincolnshire Fens made quite an impression on him, for both good and bad reasons. In his travelogue, "A Tour Through the Whole Island of Great Britain" he wrote about "wonderful engines for throwing up water… such as are not to be seen anywhere else, whereof one in particular threw up twelve hundred ton of water in half an hour, and goes by wind-sails, twelve wing or sails to a mill."

The early windmills were wooden structures, usually with four sails, though the one that so impressed Mr. Defoe close to Spalding in Lincolnshire, clearly had more. They were built on piles driven through the peat into the underlying clay, and water was lifted from one level to another by a scoop wheel inside an external brick trough. While there was a good wind blowing they were very efficient, lifting large volumes of water at a time. Unfortunately, they could only work as well as the strength of wind permitted. Because of this, on average a mill could only work one day in five, which greatly reduced their reliability. (Later, the design was to be significantly improved, using steam rather than wind to fuel the mills, but such improvements were not to arrive in time for the people of the eighteenth century.)

Windmills alone were not enough to solve the problem of moving the water over the silt at the edge of the Wash. The outfall was still very sluggish and a new channel was badly needed. A scheme proposed by Charles Kinderley in

1720 for such a channel was turned down, despite the desperation of the situation. Things were now so bad that there was not even sufficient depth in the river for ships to reach Wisbech from the sea. Tall ships carrying cargo headed for Wisbech had to be unloaded by lighters out in the Wash, a situation that was far from satisfactory. It took a further twenty years of planning before Charles' son Nathaniel was permitted to carry out work, then even longer for the work to be completed. Finally, in 1773 work began, but the Nene was channelled for a further four miles only. Beyond this point there was still no clear course through the silt, so the results, although encouraging, were only part of the solution.

The long delays in making these vital improvements seem very short-sighted. River trade by this time was of huge importance to the region, with timber, coal, iron, potash, pitch, tar and wine being amongst the goods imported through Wisbech. Crucially, exports were also numerous, among them linseed oil, firkins of butter and oats to London, with wheat being shipped along the coast to Yorkshire.

During this time, passenger craft were also using the river. Records show that there was a regular passenger route between Peterborough and Wisbech. In 1791 boats were leaving Peterborough Quay each Friday morning for Wisbech, returning before noon on Sunday.

Despite the long delay in sorting out the highly important outflow of the Nene into the Wash, progress was being made at a different part of the river. For centuries the old Well Stream from Outwell had been dwindling until it was no more than a trickle and there was no longer any access to the River Ouse from Wisbech. In 1796 a new canal was opened, roughly following the course of the old Well Stream and linking with the Nene at Wisbech. This new canal reintroduced a link with the Ouse, a facility that had been lost centuries before, and it greatly improved communication with other parts of Cambridgeshire, as well as with Norfolk and Suffolk.

Meanwhile, Wisbech went on waiting for improvements to the river's route to the sea. It would have to wait until the next century for any relief, but the port survived, managing the best it could until finally things improved in the 1830s.

Flooded Welney Washes give an indication of Fenland before drainage

The Ever-Changing Face of the Fens

However vital a role the river has played in the life of Fenland towns like Wisbech, the role of the Fen itself has always been as important. The benevolence or cruelty of the weather, the success or failure of crops, fishing and wildfowling, the welfare of livestock, the gathering of peat for fuel or reeds for roofing, all had a direct impact on the livelihood of the people, as well as a knock-on effect on the town and its commerce. Like the river, the Fens have been constantly reshaped and re-engineered, changing livelihoods and affecting communities with every new scheme throughout their long history. To understand this ancient relationship between the vast open country and the towns nurtured by it, we need to go back and take a brief look into the past.

Long before the Fens had been drained, huge areas were under water for much of the year, with the earliest villages developing, as previously mentioned, on small clay islands in the watery peat. Towns such as Ely, March and Ramsey were some of these islands. They were isolated for much of the year, impossible to reach except by boat and very few outsiders wished to brave the damp and murky conditions.

The generations of hardy Fenmen who made this area home had developed the ability to survive in these dank conditions through fishing and using their wits. They became skilled at using stilts to make their way over flooded land in summer and skates over frozen rivers and meres in winter.

Settlements such as Wisbech and Tydd had grown up as pockets of habitation on the silt fen, rather than peat, along the edge of the then much larger Wash. The isolation and hardships they experienced were similar to those encountered in the island settlements. Fog, mist and constant damp, together with the stagnant pools of water that remained even after the floods had receded, and that led all too often to sickness such as marsh fever, were all part of the life they led. Yet there were benefits too. The Fen was a source of both plentiful food and goods that could be traded. Reeds, sedge, willow and turfs were cut and could be sold on. Ducks, teal, widgeon, swans and geese were among the waterfowl that were there in plenty, as well as fish such as pike, perch, dace, bream and eels. The lush summer pasture was good for grazing in summer and in winter the hunting of wildfowl provided a good source of meat and feathers. Fenmen, for all their lack of worldly wealth, usually slept on a feather bed!

Even by 1724, when Daniel Defoe was travelling through the Fens and a great deal had been done to improve life there, he wrote that he longed to be delivered from the fogs and stagnant air and from water the colour of brewed ale!

The people of the Fens had to be tough and resilient to survive, to withstand the constant battering by nature, by politics and by their fellow man. Theirs is a long and often troubled history. Prominent in any tale from the Fens is the subject of drainage, because it was a constant battle that was never really won and brought with it so much upheaval, not all of it good for the Fenmen. Yet without it, Fenland would still be mostly under water and the thousands of acres of productive farmland that spread across it now, could never have existed.

The earliest attempts to drain small areas of low lying land are thought to be Roman, such as Car Dyke, which ran along the western edge of the Fens. Such early schemes would have enabled more crops to be grown in summer, but the problems with flooding were too overwhelming for any one scheme to make much impact.

Centuries later, with the Bishops of Ely running things from Wisbech Castle, there was a far more concentrated effort to improve the effectiveness of the Fens. Successive Bishops made attempts throughout the medieval period to improve the drainage situation, such as the highly successful Morton's Leam mentioned earlier. However, flooding of local areas was a constant menace, ruining crops and pasture. Even where a scheme was successful in improving drainage of the fields in summer, winter would inevitably bring back the flood water, as would the worst of the summer storms.

It wasn't until the seventeenth century that large scale drainage schemes were carried out. A Dutchman called Cornelius Vermuyden, brought from Holland his experience in draining low lying land, and in partnership with the Earl of Bedford and a group of investors called the Adventurers, he began the work.

He understood that the best way to drain the land was to cut long, straight channels to take the water from the previously meandering rivers. This meant the distance the channelled water had to travel was much shorter, and the gradient much increased, so that the flow of water into the sea was much greater. Increased flow also meant that the natural scouring effect of the water on the river bed was greater, further improving matters. The first phase of work began in 1631 and included the twenty one mile cut of the Old Bedford River from Earith to Salter's Lode. The work was effective over a large area, much more successful than any previous scheme, but could still only prevent floods in summer. Each winter the floods returned, so Vermuyden worked on a second phase of improvements that was to begin twenty years later.

The phase that began in 1651 included seven major works and was to have an enormously positive impact on drainage. The improvements included the cutting of the New Bedford River parallel to the old course between Earith and Denver, completion of a parallel cut to Morton's Leam between Peterborough and Guyhirn, the new Forty Foot Drain from Ramsey to Welches Dam, the Sixteen Foot Drain at Upwell, (which drained the central Fen around Chatteris and March) and the construction of two sluices, at Earith and at Denver.

As well as making a huge improvement to drainage across a very wide area, the visual impact of these new channels and sluices must have been overwhelming. The sight of broad, straight, freshly dug channels cutting across acres of what had once been marshes, reed beds and dykes, must have provoked mixed feelings as well as bringing mixed blessings. The improvements were obvious to many. A wider range of crops, such as wheat and barley, could now be grown successfully, but there were many Fen people who had only ever known a life based on a marshland economy; wildfowling, willow and reed cutting, sheep farming and fishing. They were hardly likely to welcome such massive change, especially when the Adventurers who had funded the drainage scheme were rewarded with great swathes of newly drained land, cutting across any previous rights local people might have had.

'Oh let the frogs and miry bogs destroy where they do enter'

The Fenman's hatred of this new situation was no secret. An anonymous poem survives from the time, which is known as 'Powte's Complaint,' (a powte being an old name for an eel). It describes the Fenman's fear and horror of the new schemes which he felt would destroy his future. One line describes what the poet would have liked to see happen to the developers.

"Oh let the frogs and miry bogs destroy where they do enter."

There were several violent protests by local people, in which the newly dug earth banks and drainage works were attacked as fast as they could be built. These protests were never going to make any long term difference, however. Laws governing Enclosure made it perfectly legal for the once common land of the Fens to be transferred into new ownership and enclosed. The old common rights of local people, to graze their animals, fish, gather reeds or hunt wildfowl on this land came to an abrupt halt. Yet, despite the futility of their protests, the 'Fen Tigers,' as they were starting to be called, were at least making their feelings known and refusing to give up without a fight.

In 1663, as mentioned earlier, the Bedford Level Corporation was created to look after the newly drained Fen. However, due to the high costs of repairs, and despite the obvious advantages to landowners, the regular work that was essential to maintain the channels was often neglected for years at a time. This led to a gradual deterioration of the waterways, despite some local attempts to patch up and repair areas that were getting out of control. Sadly, no further major improvements would be seen until the nineteenth century, which meant that Wisbech in the late Georgian age was surrounded by land still blighted by seasonal flooding. Records show that in 1778 local farmers had to row through their orchards in boats to collect fruit from their trees.

The modern Fens, with their backbone of drainage channels and sluices, have become a vitally important agricultural region of the country. By Georgian times there was still much work to be done, but the flat landscape surrounding the Fenland town of Wisbech was even then part of its identity, and new ideas for drainage were always being discussed.

The Smarts c.1918. L to R. Benjamin, Agnes (my Grandmother), Annie Smart, nee Negus (my Great Grandmother) and Leonard

On a personal note, I have always felt a strong connection with the Fens. I may be considered a townie, but both sides of my family were Fen people, Dad coming from the silt Fen around Wisbech, Mum from the black peat Fen of

Ramsey. Her mother was a Smart, a direct descendant of the well known Turkey Smart, one of the champion Fen skaters of the 1880s. My parents' memories, and those of their parents and grandparents, formed part of my upbringing. Apart from skaters, there had been generations of blacksmiths, farm labourers and even pumping station engineers in the family.

I have very clear and fond memories of travelling from Peterborough to visit my grandparents in Ramsey. We visited in all seasons, yet for some reason those drives across the Fen at Christmas stand out the most clearly in my mind.

Sitting in the back of Dad's Ford Cortina with my little brother, I used to gaze out of the window as we followed the lonely, narrow road that zigzagged between the stark, black fields. The ploughed earth seemed to go on forever, spreading in all directions towards a horizon so distant that it hardly existed. It was interrupted only by the occasional pale farm house, its bricks turned green by the damp that pervaded everything. You could see it rising, that cold winter damp, lifting like wraiths from the black soil and drifting across the fields. The other-worldliness of it all was enchanting and even as we arrived at Ramsey, driving through the Christmas tree decorated Great Whyte, the Fen made no effort to retreat. It was everywhere, saturating the town itself.

Staying sometimes overnight at my grandparents' house, I used to open the bedroom curtains in the morning and look out at the vast expanse of farmland that spread beyond the garden at the back of the house. At times, the wind howled unimpeded across the open acres, gathering speed until it rammed against the window panes. I was never afraid of it, just exhilarated, as any child can be who doesn't have to worry about the window panes.

It certainly doesn't affect everyone in that way. Strangers to the area often condemn the flatness as unworthy of interest. Others positively loathe it. Yet now, as in the time when Peckover House was inhabited by merchants and the Georgian port of Wisbech was teeming with activity and prosperity, the Fens are impossible to ignore. Forever changing, they are the landscape and the skyscape that give the Fenland towns their unmistakable character.

Chapter Five

Small Kingdom in a Changing World

Fenlanders have always felt a sense of isolation from the rest of the country. Centuries of struggles to keep that all important balance between flood and fertile pasture, against changing laws, politics and nature herself, have meant that they value their toughness, resilience and independence. At times believed by outsiders to have webbed feet and known as Fen Tigers, Fen people have often seen themselves as a race apart. They have long been fiercely proud and mistrustful of strangers, and poor communication and road links to the rest of the country have not helped. Yet the Fens are very much a part of England. Whatever changes and influences England, eventually arrives to shape the Fens too, and this was never more so than during the eighteenth century.

George of Hanover, who spoke little English, had come to the throne in 1714 and three more Georges were to follow him, covering more than a hundred years of British history. It was to be an age that introduced the first prime minister, Robert Walpole, a new Poor Law and the introduction of workhouses, the industrial revolution and advances in agriculture, with inventions such as Jethro Tull's seed drill, to name but a few of the influences that were shaping the country at that time. The country itself was undergoing great change; politically, economically and socially. It is a regrettable fact that much of the country's wealth was due to the slave trade, which was to endure until 1807 when campaigners such as William Wilberforce and Wisbech born Thomas Clarkson succeeded in effecting its abolition.

But what was the England of that time like? How did it differ for rich and for poor, in town and the country? How did they dress? How did they eat, play, work and get about? Having looked at life in the small town of Wisbech in East Anglia, it is time to open things out and look at the wider influences of life in England as a whole.

What the Georgians Wore

As in any age, fashion dictated what people wore and when they wore it and during the long Georgian age the line and shape of clothing for both men and women underwent several distinct changes.

In the 1720s, when the Stone family was living on North Brink, the fashionable lady's appearance would have been a time-consuming matter that relied heavily on the care and attention of her maid. The gown, petticoats, hoops and other smaller accessories had to be fitted together over her chemise and arranged on her body to create a corseted, wide-skirted shape with a loosely falling saque back to the gown. The saque back, which was to remain a part of formal dress until the 1770s, was a loosely fitting trailing section of a gown that flowed straight from the shoulders to the hem, displaying the beauty and quality of the silk. In comparison, the bodice was closely fitted at the front with a low neckline and sleeves that were fitted to just above the elbow, then fanned out into a full, lacy cuff. The hoops worn beneath the skirt gave the gown a wide-skirted, bell-shaped appearance.

The 1760s introduced side-hoops, replacing the earlier rounded ones, and these were worn over the hips to give an exaggerated wide shape. The resulting width of gowns could hinder a lady's ability to walk through narrow spaces, so hinged frames were invented, which lifted the hoops when necessary! A pair of pockets was tied under the skirt around the waist, with corresponding side openings in the gown so that a lady could easily reach them. The bodice of the gown was open at the front by this time, revealing the triangular shaped, decorated silk stomacher and a low neckline softened by silk or linen lace. The skirt also opened to display a quilted or embroidered petticoat.

Throughout this period a lady's hair was powdered, at first arranged close to the head under a small frilled cap. However, by the 1770s the powdered hairstyle was becoming more and more elaborate, arranged over a tall frame and dressed with false ringlets, feathers, jewellery and even small model boats! Once the style was complete, it was said to last for three weeks, but fortunately wigs could be worn instead. Already set, dressed and ready for wear, they saved all those hours of styling. To complete the look, the use of face powder, paint and patches was at the height of fashion. These small patches were useful for covering pock marks and other skin blemishes, but were also used wherever the wearer thought they looked most appealing and were produced in all sorts of shapes; stars, moons and flowers to name but a few.

Silk, cotton or kid mittens were worn and a light, slender fan was carried. Stockings (always white for formal dress) were gartered at the knee. Shoes were of leather or fabric with slender heels and as yet, soles were not shaped for right or left feet. A lady's shoes were so delicate that they had to be protected for outdoor wear by adding wooden soled pattens. A hooded cloak was worn as protection against the cold. Later, the calash was introduced; a voluminous collapsible silk hood over a frame, which covered the hairstyle out of doors.

From the 1780s the line of gowns changed completely. A slimmer shape came in, supported at the back of the skirt by a bustle. The robe was closed at the front and although the neckline was still low, it was filled with a folded muslin neckerchief. Riding coat-dresses were popular, worn with a jacket and a hat set forward on the brow. Hair was still dressed high on the head but was less often powdered during the day and by the end of the 1780s, powder was discarded altogether.

Yet the greatest change to fashion came at the end of the century. Out went the hoops, bustles, stays and tight bodices of previous fashion and in came slender, draping dresses, inspired by ancient Greece. The new gowns were high waisted with a fairly low neckline, the long, clinging muslin skirts trailing to the ground. White was a very popular 'colour', with linens and muslins being plain or spotted. In cooler weather a Kashmir shawl was worn, and like muslin, was introduced to British taste by the country's growing interests in India.

Hair was kept to its natural colour and was arranged in soft curls, later coiled up on the head. Turbans or ostrich feathers were very fashionable, and reticules were carried along with a fan. Reticules, the silken and embroidered forerunners of modern handbags, were needed now that inner pockets could no longer be hidden under the voluminous skirts of previous times.

This fine fashion, of course, was only enjoyed by the higher social orders. For working women, a gown of coarse cloth was worn with a petticoat, shift, apron and stockings, with a cap covering the hair. For those even further down the social scale, a separate skirt and bodice were the norm, with the bodice supported by bone or wooden stays. Stays had been an everyday part of the poor woman's costume since the 1500s and since they could not be washed, would have become ever dirtier and more uncomfortable with the years.

Staffordshire pottery figures showing fashion of the 1750s

Gentlemen's fashion was dictated by the same influences as women's. In the 1720s, while the ladies of the house were being dressed by their maids, the Stone brothers would have been dressed in the distinctive long, full skirted, buttoned coat of that time. With its large pocket flaps and wide cuffs, the coat was worn over a long, embroidered waistcoat, which was left unbuttoned from the waist to the hem and tightened at the back with tapes. The cuffs were cut slightly short at the wrist to display the lace of the shirt sleeves. Breeches were worn to the knee in a close fitting style, with stockings of black or coloured silk gartered below the knee.

During the 1720s the huge, curled periwig remained in fashion, but by 1730 younger men were beginning to favour a shorter styled wig, which was twisted at the back to form a long ringlet.

Shoes were round-toed with small heels and large buckles, with boots being used for riding only. Thick, loosely cut, cloth overcoats had large collars and cuffs, while hats remained in the one style that had been favoured for years; the three cornered or tri-corn hat. These were made of black beaver and generally trimmed with braid or lace.

From 1735 the stock came into fashion and remained for several decades. This was a folded neckband, which was fastened at the back and allowed the ruffled front of the shirt to be displayed at the open front of the waistcoat.

By 1760 coats had taken on a slimmer shape, the front curving gradually away towards the back. Cuffs were smaller, but still displayed shirt frills at the wrist.

As with the ladies, the 1790s brought in a completely new style. Fashionable gentlemen discarded their wigs and had their hair cut shorter and brushed forward over the forehead. This gave a look of casual untidiness that was becoming a popular affectation with the young. Tri-corn hats were outdated at last, replaced by tall crowned, wide brimmed beaver hats, which would later develop into top hats.

The coat was cut to a completely new shape; cut square across the front at waist height, with longer sides and back that reached the knees. Often made from velvet, it was double breasted with a high, overturned collar. It was worn over a short waistcoat and shirt with a linen stock that reached high on the neck. Breeches were replaced by the new pantaloons, which were ankle length and tight fitting.

Working men typically wore cast-off coats with second hand waistcoats and breeches. Woollen stockings, a stout coat, strong shoes, a coarse linen shirt, a neck-cloth and hat usually completed their wardrobe. Until the end of the century wigs, which could be bought second hand, usually formed part of the costume.

Elegantly, adequately, or poorly dressed, according to status, the townspeople of Wisbech and of every town throughout Britain went about their business. The poor worked and the better-off mixed duty with pleasure. But what were these pleasures? How did the well-heeled people of Georgian England play?

How the Georgians Played

With their everyday needs looked after by servants, the genteel eighteenth century family had the time and liberty to enjoy all the fine things in life that the Georgian age presented.

For the educated lady at home there was plenty that was deemed suitable for her entertainment. Reading, needlework, country walks, music and dance were all encouraged. For gentlemen, there was a greater variety of diversions. Many sports, foreign travel, as well as the walking, music and dance shared with the ladies, were open to them. It was a time of great development in the arts, with theatre buildings evolving into the covered stage, backstage and audience seating format we would find familiar today, with a complex system of ropes, pulleys and trap doors, all of them working with magical speed to effect scenery changes. Theatres had been a part of London life for centuries, but now the demand for purpose-built theatres was reaching the provinces. This can be seen in Wisbech, where previously a barn had been used for a touring playgroup's production and where in 1793 a specially built theatre, complete with traps and gadgets, was opened to greet a more demanding audience.

The early eighteenth century was greatly influenced by the Baroque style and the painting, music and sculpture created at this time were to make their mark throughout the whole century. It was a new, flamboyant style which used dramatic and unrestrained shapes and forms. Many composers' new works were influenced by the Baroque and new musical forms, such as opera, the concerto and the sonata were created at this time. Bach, Purcell, Monteverdi and Pachelbel were among the composers producing grand pieces, with works like Vivaldi's 'The Four Seasons' (1723) and Handel's 'Water Music Suite' (1717) still well known and loved today. Later in the century, Wolfgang and Anna Mozart, the Austrian child prodigies, visited England and played a musical composition written by the nine year old Wolfgang. His operas, piano concertos, sonatas and symphonies were to become some of the best loved music of all time.

Artists such as Thomas Gainsborough, Johann Zoffany and Joshua Reynolds were all in demand to paint portraits of the wealthy, who could also enjoy Gainsborough's landscapes or George Stubbs' horse paintings. Less palatable were the satirical works of William Hogarth. He depicted life as he saw it across all classes, showing vices and degradation in a way that must have made uncomfortable viewing for some. He created series of engravings, one of which, 'Marriage a la Mode' shows the gradual decline of an arranged aristocratic marriage with just about every tragic ingredient of a modern soap thrown in.

At home, playing the piano and singing to entertain a family or small social group was considered a highly important accomplishment for both gentlemen and women. The leisured classes took their entertainment very seriously and the long winter evenings were often filled with singing, dancing and card playing.

Dance was a very important part of social life that could reach across all classes. Popular dances of the day, often held in public assembly rooms and large private houses, still followed the traditional English Country Dance format, using two lines of dancers, made up of pairs facing each other. One of the most popular dances was the 'Sir Roger de Coverley'. For two people there was also the graceful minuet, danced to music by Handel or Bach. The poorer members of a community were more likely to be working than dancing at these occasions and found far fewer opportunities to dance themselves, but village celebrations for weddings and harvest festivals are legendary.

The sporting world was a lively one, with many of the activities we know so well today becoming established. Others, such as bear-baiting and cock-fighting, however popular, thankfully have died out. Bowls and cricket, far gentler sports, were played on open pasture and village greens. In 1787 Thomas Lord opened a new cricket club at Dorset Fields, London, where teams from around the country would compete with the Gentlemen Players, distinguishable by their white top hats with black bands. From this beginning, and after two changes of venue, the Marylebone Cricket Club grew into the world famous club that it is today, with its equally celebrated ground at Lords.

The playing of golf is thought to go back centuries, but when the first Rules of Golf were published at St. Andrews in 1758 the game's popularity rapidly grew and remained a favourite for gentlemen. Football's origins are thought to go back to the 1500s in England, where any gathering of boys, using a pig's bladder or anything else resembling a ball would be kicked about, using early versions of the rules that are followed now. The earliest football clubs, though, would not be formed until the next century, when it would develop into a popular spectator sport. A different kind of spectator sport much enjoyed by gentlemen was boxing, with the Championship of England being a hotly contested title. Horse racing was also well followed, with race meetings held throughout the country. The first racing calendar appeared for the Newmarket races in 1727, and in 1752 the Jockey Club was founded to establish rules for British racing.

Guiseppe Baretti, the Italian I mentioned earlier who visited Wisbech in 1778/79, wrote enthusiastically about much of the town's entertainment and mentioned playing cards, going on morning and evening walks, as well as attending balls and suppers. The event he seems to have enjoyed most of all was Race Week, which was held at a stadium in Emneth, close to the Downham Road. He described the horses, jockeys and the races themselves and seems to have loved the atmosphere. He described, "...the vociferations of the bystanders and the universal clapping of hands...added to these the invitations so many make to lay wagers. The ladies...do not know how to restrain themselves and resist the general mania of betting and thus they wager amongst each other for a pot of coffee..." The bets laid by the men, however, went a bit further than coffee, with considerable sums of money changing hands.

The benefits of exercise were well understood by this time, the old ignorance that had led people to believe that walking was harmful to women and the elderly, at last corrected. As a result, both sexes enjoyed countryside walking and for men, running, weight training as well as exercise in early gymnasia, was not unknown.

For the less energetic, board games such as chess were well loved, as was the card game of Whist, the forerunner of Bridge. Cards, which had blank backs and no Jokers, were a useful diversion for the more senior members of a community at social events, who could spend happy hours around a Whist table while the young were dancing.

Reading was strongly encouraged to educate the mind. The art of conversation amongst polite society was greatly prized and the more you read, the more informed you were likely to be and a better conversationalist. Reading material was becoming more varied, with the novel having developed into the form we know today. Novels were immensely popular, such as Daniel Defoe's adventure story, 'Robinson Crusoe' (1719) and sentimental tales, like Oliver Goldsmith's 'The Vicar of Wakefield' (1766). One genre which was taking the literary world by storm was the Gothic novel, such as Horace Walpole's 'The Castle of Otranto' (1764). With its spooky atmosphere and pleasurable thrill, it was the forerunner of the modern horror story.

An absolute must for the young gentleman and woman of fashion during this time was the season in the spa town of Bath. Centred around taking the spa waters, the entertainment included dancing, dining, the theatre, as well as mornings spent in gossip in the pump rooms. Bath was the place to be seen and to meet new acquaintances and was one of the high points in the social calendar for the leisured classes.

One pastime for wealthy young men of this era, and one of the greatest influences on his education and development, came through the Grand Tour. After a university education a young gentleman would typically travel through France and Italy in search of art and culture. Often with almost unlimited funds and aristocratic connections wherever he went, he could travel for months or even years, commissioning works of art and perfecting his use of Italian and French. It was a kind of rite of passage for a gentleman of means and many noble houses became enriched with paintings and sculpture brought home from such tours.

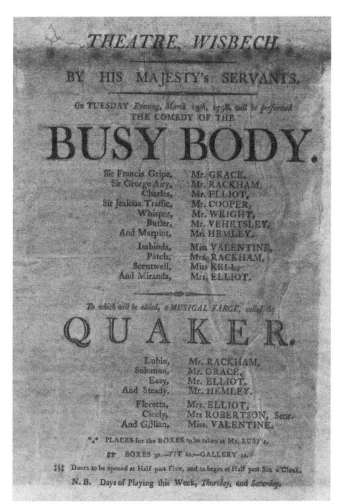

An early playbill from The Theatre, Wisbech (with kind permission of Wisbech and Fenland Museum)

How the Georgians Worked

At the other end of the scale, labouring Britain was going at full steam. Whether in agriculture, industry, or in service, the lower classes of Britain were hard at work, enduring long hours and little pay.

Agriculture and Life on the Land

Until the laws governing the enclosure of common land made their impact on the countryside, peasants had the right to graze their animals on open common pasture. This ancient right of access to the common helped people to eke out a living based on poor farm wages. Some of the very poorest peasants called 'squatters' even lived on the common, in shacks. When lords of the manor became entitled by Parliament during the early eighteenth century to sell off this common land, in order to increase the size of their farms or to build factories and houses, these old rights came to an end. The poor who were unable to find work on the enlarged farms began to leave the villages, heading for the cities in search of work. In some cases whole villages were abandoned, yet the enclosure of common land continued for much of the century.

Meanwhile, land owners were becoming more influential and their farms more efficient. One of the greatest influences on farming was the university educated Jethro Tull. His newly invented Seed Drill was hugely successful. Whereas in the past seed had been broadcast by hand from baskets, the Seed Drill sowed seeds in straight lines at uniform depth and intervals before covering the seed with earth. This invention boosted crops everywhere. Jethro Tull went on to publish 'The Horse Hoing Husbandry', a series of essays explaining his new approach to farming. This too was eagerly received by farmers, but his Mechanical Hoe was less of a success, despite its claim to weed efficiently between lines of seedlings.

Another significant development came in the new four course crop rotation system devised by Charles, Viscount 'Turnip' Townsend. He was a former Whig politician who farmed in Norfolk and his new method of using a four year sequence of crop planting eliminated the old and wasteful practice of leaving one field in three fallow. The four crops of clover, wheat, turnips and barley replenished the soil with the necessary nutrients to begin the cycle again. The turnips were used to feed cattle in winter, ending the previous practice of having to slaughter the animals each autumn. This huge breakthrough is what gave the viscount his nick name of 'Turnip'.

Industry

In the cities, especially in the north and the Midlands, there was no shortage of work, however bad the conditions may have been. Weaving was still England's major industry in the early 1700s, providing the largest export. Cotton was imported from India and woven in Lancashire into calicoes or fustian (a mixture of linen and cotton). Printed cotton fabrics were very fashionable and this demand kept the industry buoyant for decades, with one of the most lucrative export markets being the American colonies.

By the mid-1700s industry of all kinds was rapidly expanding. Ironware and pottery were in production in and around Birmingham, where villages were growing into small towns, bloated with the expanding urban population. Josiah Wedgewood and other potters were flourishing in Stoke on Trent, as methods of producing pottery and porcelain were being refined. The production of iron was also being developed, in that it could now be smelted using coke, rather than charcoal as before. As a result, ironworks could be moved closer to the Midland coalfields, away from their old locations by the forests. In 1762 a factory producing buttons, buckles and other small metal items opened in Birmingham, making good use of this new advance in technology. Other cities in the Midlands were equally productive, as can be seen from Daniel Defoe's comments, written while visiting Coventry. He described it as, "a large and populous city and drives a very good trade; the manufacture of tammies [a glazed woollen fabric used for undergarments and linings] is their chief employ and next to that weaving of ribbons of the meanest kind, chiefly black."

By 1769 the term 'Industrial Revolution' was being used and a survey of the time showed some of the industry that was reshaping the cities. In Rotherham the coal mines employed around five hundred people. In the same town there were foundries forging boilers and ploughshares. In Sheffield there were iron and steel mills, also a plate works producing silver table ware. In Newcastle upon Tyne there were coal mines, in Crawley ironworks, and rather disturbingly, in Warrington there was a pin factory employing 200-300 children. In Manchester the cotton mills were known to employ entire families.

In Lancashire the textile industry was expanding at a huge rate. A deep water canal had been dug in the earlier part of the century to link the fast growing commercial centres of Liverpool and Manchester. The old situation where workers used a simple spinning wheel in their own cottage was no longer viable in this fast developing industry. Houses were being turned into small factories and villages into small towns in the industrial north.

In periods of great and sudden change there usually comes a backlash and in the cotton industry it was sparked by the Spinning Jenny. This ingenious yet heartbreaking piece of machinery was invented by James Hargreaves and could drive a whole line of spindles at once, replacing the need for dozens of individual spinning wheels. In one move, the old cottage industry came well and truly to an end. Spinners who faced the loss of their income reacted violently, smashing the hated machines wherever they found them. Despite this, progress was unstoppable.

Steam engines had already been invented and were used to drive some machines, but James Watt invented the condenser, which made steam engines more efficient by condensing the compressed steam. This advance led to a greater and wider use of machines in all parts of industry.

The pump at Peckover; handy for the weekly wash

Domestic Work

A huge proportion of the working population of Britain at that time was employed neither in agriculture nor in industry, but in service in private houses. Even moderately sized homes of middle class professionals employed one or two servants. A gentleman's household, even with a

modest income, employed a cook at the very least, with an additional maid or manservant in many cases. The need for domestic servants in every town and village meant a huge demand for young people to enter service. And young they were. Working families often needed their children to begin earning as soon as possible, so many scullery maids or hall boys entered service by the age of ten, though this could be as young as eight.

A household the size of Peckover in Wisbech is likely to have required between eight and twelve servants in order to run the house and grounds efficiently. By the mid 1700s the Southwell family was in residence and they are likely to have needed a housekeeper, butler, coachman, cook, lady's maid, housemaid, scullery maid, groom and gardeners, with outside help to do additional work as necessary. There was a clearly defined hierarchy amongst the servants, ranging from the housekeeper and butler at the top, to the most lowly scullery maid or hall boy. The eighteenth century home, relying so heavily on its servants, was not a private place for anyone living there. Servants had to be summoned by ringing a hand bell, a sound that did not carry far, meaning that an attendant would always have to be within earshot, ready for any summons. The system of pulleys to connect bells with distant service areas was not to be introduced until the next century, when servants would be able to be kept more at a distance.

All servants in an eighteenth century household rose early, with the scullery maid usually the first up at five o/clock, responsible for lighting the kitchen fire ready for washing and breakfast cooking. She would also have carried out menial kitchen jobs, such as preparing fruit and vegetables for cooking, washing up and scrubbing clean the working areas. Outside help would also be employed and in a house the size of Peckover it was usual for a laundry maid from the town to come in very early on the weekly wash day.

The wash day duties in the days before modern detergents and machines, when garments were far from easy-care, were onerous. To give an illustration of the working life of a lower servant, the following is a glimpse of a laundry maid's duties.

She would arrive on duty at about five o'clock with the scullery maid and her first duty was to fill large cauldrons with water from the pump and heat them over the fire. Peckover had a conveniently placed pump just outside the servants' hall door, by the cellar entrance, so she would have had less distance to haul the heavy wooden buckets of water than maids in less modern and well equipped houses. Washing a single load would have taken about fifty gallons of water, all of which had to be heated in the huge cauldrons over the fire, then ladled into wooden wash tubs on stools or tables. Any linen items had to be soaked overnight before being added to the wash tubs of boiling water, together with cotton and muslin shifts and underclothes, all of which were normally washed once a week. These fabrics were hard wearing and could take the harsh weekly treatment of boiling and pounding. The maid would scrub the items by hand, using a washboard and soap made with lye, a mixture of wood ash and urine. The lye was irritating to the hands, causing many a skin problem, and stooping over the boiling pans and carrying hot water from place to place was back breaking work. By 1785 a primitive three legged appliance called a 'dolly', was used to turn the clothes in the tub in order to avoid developing yellow spots on the fabric from the lye. The laundry was then lifted out of the tub with a stick, rinsed twice and wrung out before hanging out to dry.

Other fabrics were cleaned a lot less often. Woollen garments had to be washed separately in cold water to avoid shrinking, so tended to be laundered altogether every few weeks. The fine gowns worn by the mistress were cleaned even more rarely. Before any washing could be done, the lady's maid had to remove all the buttons and lace from the garment, unpicking the seams to separate the different layers of silk and lace, so that each piece could be given the care it needed.

When the day's laundry was dry, the great piles of ironing had to be dealt with. The laundry maid used a box iron with removable iron billets inside it, which were regularly removed and reheated on the fire.

Depending on how many days she worked or whether she was regularly employed in one of the larger houses, a laundry maid would have earned around £5 per year.

Other Types of Work

As well as the working classes, there were also the more educated and privileged, yet far from idle classes, who followed some kind of profession. It was usual in wealthy or even titled families for the eldest son to inherit the title, lands and great house, while younger sons went into the army, navy or the church. Further down the social scale came the merchants and farming landowners, and with the coming of the industrial age, the factory and pit owners. There was also the medical profession, with a local doctor situated close to most villages and in the towns. There were advances being made in surgery too, though the work was treated with suspicion. Body snatchers, as they were known, illegally dug up recently buried bodies and sold them to hospitals for research. However grisly, it was vital research that led to gradual advances in surgery.

Journalism as a profession enjoyed a boom time in the eighteenth century, with writers enjoying considerable freedom of speech and able to hire themselves out to the newspapers of the day. Many successful men began their careers in journalism, such as Daniel Defoe, Jonathan

Swift and Samuel Johnson. 'The Tatler' was set up in 1709 to publish the news and gossip from the London coffee houses and the number of newspapers in print rapidly increased to meet the demands of an educated public. By the 1780s the two most popular newspapers were 'The Times' (previously called 'The Daily Universal Register') and 'The Morning Chronicle', which published racing results as well as daily news, even advertisements, such as where the music lover could buy Mozart's latest musical score.

How Georgian Children Played…or Didn't

Never was the gulf between rich and poor in Georgian England so marked as in the treatment of children. Despite this, in the early 1700s the modern concept of a childhood spent in play was as foreign to the rich as it was to the poor.

Fortunately, the Georgian period was to be one of significant change in the education and raising of children. In the early part of the century it was still considered that childhood was nothing more than training for adulthood, when a child's unruly nature should be suppressed as early as possible. Children of the wealthy were still dressed like miniature adults and expected to act accordingly. Paintings of the time showed stiff and formal family groups, with the usually stern-faced father, as provider and disciplinarian, in the centre. Traditional thinking led parents to discourage play and affectionate behaviour from the age of seven, which was considered to be the time of the 'onset of reason'.

However, change was coming. One of the most influential thinkers of the 1750s and 60s was Jean-Jacques Rousseau, who considered that children should be permitted much more freedom. He understood that they needed to be able to run around and play until the age of twelve, in order to develop physical strength. He also believed that they would better learn to tell right from wrong through experiencing the consequences of their actions, rather than by punishment. His ideas were revolutionary at the time, but gradually became accepted by society.

Although most of Rousseau's advice was aimed at the upper classes, his influence gradually reached all levels. More and more children were at last receiving rudimentary education. England was still behind the rest of Europe in terms of education, and there was a drive nationwide to provide some sort of education for all children, either free of cost or affordable. There were grammar schools in most towns, such as the one in Wisbech, which offered scholarships to local boys, who were as likely to be sons of yeomen and shop keepers as of local gentry. Poorer children were educated in the Anglican Church charity schools, but since the children often had to work to help their families, these lessons, which were focused on their spiritual well-being, were usually held only on Sundays, their one work-free day.

The sons of aristocrats, however, were not educated locally, continuing to attend the long established major schools, such as Eton, Winchester and Westminster. Girls were still taught to read, write and manage the household accounts by their mothers, no further education being considered necessary for them.

Children's books were becoming popular for those who could afford them; nursery rhymes, alphabets and readers, as well as educational games such as the 'Spelling Box'. This was created by Ellenor Fenn in 1780 as one of her many new ideas to aid child education. She, like Rousseau and others by this time, believed in a less rigid method of learning, where play, rather than discipline could be used to encourage the very young to learn. The Spelling Box consisted of a number of trays containing cards, which could be used to form sentences. Each card showed a single letter, number, picture or phrase. The mother retained control of the toy, only allowing the child to play with it when she considered him to be at his most receptive. Depending on the age of the child, he could focus on one letter, phrase or image at a time and learn to form sentences around it, tackling more complicated phrases as he grew older. An example of this toy is in the collection of Peckover House.

This era of more liberal thinking was reflected in paintings of the time, such as Hogarth's 'The Children's Party', in which the formal group of previous times was giving way to scenes of children playing freely in harmonious surroundings.

By this time something was at last being done for the very poorest children. London's Foundling Hospital was begun in 1739 by Thomas Coram and took in abandoned children. So desperate was the situation, where all too often unwanted babies were being left at roadsides or rubbish dumps, that in the first four years the hospital admitted 15,000 babies. To help raise funds, a concert was staged by the great George Frederic Handel, performing 'The Messiah' in 1750, arguably the country's first charity concert.

It was a time of profound rural hardship, with the enclosure of common land and industrialisation drawing the poor into towns. The urban life they found had its own share of ills, with children as young as six working in terrible conditions, as chimney sweeps or down mines. As mentioned earlier, a pin mill in Manchester employed around three hundred children and it was usual for some factories to employ the whole family, irrespective of age. When Daniel Defoe was travelling through Norwich he was impressed with the town which offered plenty of employment, saying, "The very children after four or five years of age could every one earn their own bread." The fact that this situation seems acceptable, even impressive to him, speaks volumes for the thinking of the times.

The first child labour laws, which would at least lay down the beginnings of improvement, would not be introduced until the 1830s; far too late to help Georgian children.

The Spelling Box (in the collection of Peckover House)

How the Georgians Ate and Drank

The middle and upper classes of the eighteenth century really enjoyed their food, sampling a great variety of dishes served at times of the day to fit a more leisured lifestyle than is usual today.

The food available to create the lavish meals served in large households still relied greatly on the season, but Georgian cooks had learned ingenious methods of preserving food. They produced candied fruit, wine, jam, as well as bottled, pickled and potted vegetables. On larger estates ice was available for most of the year from the ice house. This was a domed, sunken, brick lined store for the blocks of ice that were collected during the winter. The stored ice was then used throughout the year to make desserts. The greatest proportion of the well-heeled family's diet, however, was meat, and this could be preserved by a method called collaring. This involved salting, seasoning, then boiling the meat in a vinegar solution. It was then rolled up tightly in a cloth and steeped in vinegar until ready for use. Bread was made in most households and formed the basis of many meals, while the most usual drink was beer; much safer than the often dubious water supplies.

In upper class households the timing of meals shifted considerably during the eighteenth century. In the early 1700s dinner was eaten around 2pm, but by the end of the century it had moved to around 5pm, with the most fashionable London families delaying even later to 7pm, taking advantage of the plentiful candle light available to them.

A typical eating plan in a fashionable London household would have looked something like the following.

Breakfast was served until about 11am. It was a light meal, usually consisting of bread or muffins with coffee.

As the timing for dinner slid further back in the day, the lengthening gap between breakfast and dinner began to be filled with a snack called luncheon. This was served around midday and would have been an informal meal of whatever was to hand, usually meat and bread.

Dinner, being the main meal of the day, was the most lavish in a wealthy household. It was also the most popular time for entertaining, so the whole family would often sit down with their guests around a dinner table decked with a damask cloth, silver candelabra and a porcelain dinner service. Dinner typically consisted of three courses and on special occasions each of these courses could be made up from around twenty five separate dishes. These dishes were placed on the table all at once, with diners helping themselves to the food closest to them. Rather than sampling all the dishes on the table, each diner was only likely to eat from those nearest to him, since it was considered very impolite to keep asking for food at the other end of the table to be passed down. Because of this, a modern reader looking at a detailed Georgian menu can easily get the wrong idea that all Georgians were gluttons! At the end of each course the dishes were cleared and the next course set out. The first course typically included fresh or preserved vegetables accompanied by generous amounts of meat and poultry. Mock Turtle (a calf's head) was a popular centre piece. The second course consisted mainly of meat, such as pheasant, hare, collared pig, crayfish and snipe. The third course was made up of fairly simple desserts; mainly bottled and fresh fruits and ices.

As dinner concluded, the hostess would lead the ladies from the dining room, leaving the gentlemen to drink wine or port and discuss the politics or news of the day. Tea was then served for the ladies in a separate room, where they could appreciate the luxury of drinking this new exotic, highly expensive brew while making polite conversation. After a short time the gentlemen would join them, when cake could also be served.

If there were house guests to entertain, dancing or cards would most likely follow, with supper being served shortly before bedtime.

All this fine dining had an inevitable affect on teeth. Help was at hand, however, since false teeth could be purchased fairly easily. These were made from various materials including pearl, silver, wood, walrus teeth or recycled human teeth.

There are several surviving descriptions of menus from the time and some of the most detailed were recorded in the diary of James Woodforde, a clergyman and later a fellow of New College, Oxford. He loved to dine with friends and to take his turn in entertaining them to dinner. He describes the dinner he gave to a group of friends at his parsonage close to Norwich on August 27th 1784.

For the first course there was, "Pike, a couple of fowls boiled and Piggs Face, green peas soup and a prodigious fine and fat Haunch of Venison..." For the second course there followed, "Fricasse, a couple of Ducks roasted, green peas, plum Pudding, Macaroni..."

At Parson Woodforde's dinner was served at 3pm, but it would have lasted for several hours, taking the event well into evening. He recorded in his diary one November that he had invited a friend to one of his dinner parties, but that the friend had declined, due to having to walk home and there being no moon that night. Paths in rural areas were clearly too dangerous for travel after dark on a night with no moon.

Manners and behaviour of gentle folk up to this time had not always been known for their refinement, but by the eighteenth century a new standard of behaviour was becoming the norm. Picking one's teeth, sniffing one's food, scratching oneself, spitting, blowing one's nose and leaning one's elbows on the table were now generally frowned upon. The sexes had previously been separated at the table, but now gentlemen and ladies sat together. Even the old habit of using the chamber pot behind a screen in the dining room was under threat in this new polite era. It was now considered more acceptable if one left the room quietly, without stating one's purpose, when the need arose.

The table was set much as we would be familiar with today. Forks had only recently become part of everyday cutlery, previously considered rather unnecessary tools. By the mid eighteenth century a well-to-do table setting included a knife, fork and spoon, made of silver or the best Sheffield steel. Drinking glasses had developed into elegant shapes by this time, produced in a long tradition of English glass making. Since George Ravenscroft had introduced lead oxide into the production process in 1676, glasses had become heavier and denser in shape. With their many variations in form, they were objects of beauty. The most greatly prized things on the table, though, would have been the porcelain plates and dishes in the latest designs by factories such as Bow or Worcester.

It was the new fashion for tea drinking that had created the demand for a hard wearing ceramic that could withstand the impact of boiling water needed for tea brewing. Porcelain had been imported into Britain since the sixteenth century from the Far East, but it was very expensive and there was an increasing need for English potters to learn the secret of porcelain making for themselves. A thick, heavy type of ceramic, known as delftware, had been in use in Britain for a century or more, but it was neither fine nor durable enough for tea drinking. Research and experimentation came up with two new types of ware; pottery and porcelain. Porcelain differs from pottery in that it is generally finer and can usually be seen through when held up to the light. Pottery is much coarser and is usually opaque.

A New Hall hard paste porcelain teabowl and saucer in the 'Boy With Butterfly' pattern

The Georgian Love of Porcelain

It was not until 1710 that a European manufacturer, the Meissen factory in Dresden, discovered the secret of producing porcelain. The New Hall factory in Staffordshire followed soon afterwards, using Cornish clay in the process. Two types of porcelain were soon being produced in England, hard and soft paste, but both types were unreliable, often collapsing in the firing kiln or cracking when boiling water was poured into them. Chinese porcelain was still the best and more development was clearly required. A solution came with the substitution of soapstone for china clay in manufacture. This brought great improvements, and new factories at Worcester, Vauxhall and Caughley began to produce this new ware. An even more beneficial development came with the introduction of bone ash to the mixture. This further reduced the problem of kiln collapse and produced a whiter, more 'plastic' body. The Bow factory first produced this new bone china in 1749, followed shortly afterwards by Lowestoft and Chelsea.

Bone china was soon gracing the dining tables of the wealthy. By 1800 English porcelain had reached something close to perfection, with many excellent potteries producing fine table ware and other goods.

Pottery; the Ceramic for the Masses

Even porcelain produced in England was expensive and only the wealthy could aspire to owning it. However, a new middle class of tradesmen and artisans with disposable income was establishing itself. Although in many cases unable to afford porcelain, they still had the wish to beautify their homes and to follow fashion. A less expensive product was needed to fill this large gap in the market.

In the 1720s it was discovered that by mixing clay with ground flint, cream coloured earthenware could be produced. This had the look of porcelain and it quickly gained in popularity. Many of the first factories were in Stoke-on-Trent, later known as 'The Potteries', using white clay from Devon and Dorset. The Whieldon factory produced table wares finished with tortoiseshell-like glazes and later Josiah Wedgwood's imaginative and useful pieces, named Queen's Ware after Queen Charlotte, made creamware even more fashionable and desirable.

As well as practical items, ornamental figurines were produced in huge numbers. While factories such as Meissen in Germany and Bow in England were creating porcelain shepherdess figurines for their wealthy customers, cheaper creamware versions were produced for more modest budgets. They were mostly rural subjects, such as gardeners and haymakers, but could also be religious or classical, Elijah, Charity, Neptune or Venus being examples.

In the late eighteenth century the Staffordshire potters tried to give their wares a more refined look with a new, whiter glaze. By adding a small amount of cobalt, the glaze gained a bluish tint, resulting in a whiter finish. The new glaze, called Pearlware, gradually replaced creamware. These pieces could be decorated with coloured glazes, using copper for green, iron for yellow, manganese for brown etc. Some of the best potters were the Wood family and the Walton factory. The range of figures increased with their popularity and they became known as 'toys'. They included animal subjects, the four seasons, as well as the ever popular religious and classical subjects.

Coffee and Tea

During the period when porcelain and pottery were making their way onto Georgian tables, our favourite hot drinks of modern times were also making a niche for themselves.

Tea, coffee and chocolate had first arrived in Europe in the seventeenth century, with a new kind of establishment opening in which to drink them; the coffee house. The first one opened in England in 1650 and by 1700 they were common-place, rapidly becoming a prominent feature of eighteenth century male social life.

For a penny, a man could gain admission, with a cup of coffee, and all but the very lowest rank of society could meet there. These new establishments were quite distinct from taverns, which by law had to provide food, drink and lodging and were often centres for gambling too. In contrast, coffee houses served stimulants, not intoxicants. They prohibited gambling and alcohol, so quickly gained the reputation of being sober, genteel places. They were the domain of men only and although occasionally women worked in them, they were not permitted to patronise them.

Men met in coffee houses to discuss business, current affairs, politics and scandal. Influential thinkers and writers of the time would often meet and speak there and some of the houses began to specialise in certain subjects. Some played an important role in the development of financial markets, some in the development of newspapers. Another, owned by a Mr. Edward Lloyd, was frequented by sea captains and maritime insurers. To help his customers, Mr. Lloyd began to display notices giving the arrival and departure times of ships from the London docks. Long after his death the loyal customers of his coffee house formed the insurance company still known today as Lloyds of London. Another great institution, the London Stock Exchange, operated for seventy three years out of Jonathan's and Garraway's Coffee Houses.

In 1660 Samuel Pepys, the well known diarist of the seventeenth century, wrote about his first visit to a coffee house; "...to the Coffee House, into a room next the water by ourselves, where we spent an hour or two. Here we had variety of brave Italian and Spanish songs and a Canon for eight voices."

Tea, however, had a much more gradual introduction to the British way of life. Although tea drinking dates back to the 3rd Millennium BC in China, the first tea did not arrive in England until the mid seventeenth century. A hundred years later the East India Company was regularly importing it, but it was a very expensive commodity. As early as 1657 Thomas Garraway's Coffee House was advertising tea at a cost of £10 per pound and he had to produce a pamphlet to explain to his discerning customers what this new luxury was and how to prepare and drink it.

Tea became popular among the aristocracy when Catherine of Braganza, Charles ll's Portuguese Queen, introduced the drinking of tea to court. Its popularity soon spread to the upper and middle classes. By 1700 over five hundred coffee houses sold tea as well as coffee, upsetting the tavern owners whose gin and ale sales were going down. The government was also displeased, as it was losing tax revenue on alcohol, and to remedy this, a massive tax on tea of 119% was imposed. This inevitably led to smuggling, with ships bringing tea from Holland and smugglers hiding the contraband in safe places, such as parish churches. It wasn't until 1784 that Prime Minister William Pitt the Younger reduced the tax to 12.5%, effectively putting an end to smuggling. However, it was still very costly and practices such as mixing tea with willow or liquorish to make it go further, and re-drying used tea leaves before adding a few new ones, still went on.

Such a luxurious commodity required the very best items to drink it from. Silver teapots were used in wealthy households, together with porcelain table ware. The drinking of tea came to epitomise civilised behaviour among the upper classes, with the lady of the house keeping the tea locked in a tea caddy. Anna, seventh Duchess of Bedford is said to have started the tradition of afternoon tea and many painters of the time captured the elegance of this increasingly fashionable pastime. The earliest cups were actually 'tea bowls', handle-less cups imported from China and later produced by English factories. The fine china bowls were held between the forefinger and thumb and it was not until around 1800 that cups with handles became available and gradually replaced tea bowls.

Tea was generally thought to be good for the health. In 1667 Samuel Pepys wrote, "Home, and there find my wife making of tea, a drink which Mr. Pelling the Pottecary [Apothecary] tells her is good for her colds and defluxions."

Life in a Georgian home for anyone of adequate means was supplied with a great many comforts, therefore. But what was it like when it became necessary to leave home and travel around? How did people of the eighteenth century fare on the roads of England?

The Georgian stables at Peckover House

How the Georgians Travelled

Until the mid to late 1700s, most roads connecting the towns of Britain were little more than rutted dirt tracks, trampled by foot traffic and horses. As soon as the autumn rains began, road surfaces were reduced to mud, and travel effectively ceased until the spring. When conditions allowed, most travellers made their way on foot or on horseback. Heavy loads, such as timber or stone for building and industry, had either to be moved by canal or were transported by trains of pack horses, because loaded wagons were too heavy and were quickly mired down in the mud.

Despite the poor state of the roads, people of the time seemed pretty stoic about riding or walking long distances. Parson Woodforde, the clergyman mentioned earlier and who recorded so much of everyday life in his diaries, made several references to making journeys into town, often in poor weather. His parsonage was ten miles from Norwich and in February 1792 he recorded that he "sent Briton early this morning on horseback to Norwich after News and many other things. He came home about 5 o'clock…it snowed the whole day with a strong wind and also froze sharply all day." Briton was his man servant, who seems to have made the twenty mile round trip for the parson every week.

For longer journeys, travelling by stage coach had been possible for centuries, but there were no regular routes and early coaches were little more than lumbering covered wagons. Journeys in them had been painfully slow. In 1706 the situation had improved somewhat, with a regular route between London and York being established, and other routes soon following. The construction of the stage coach itself had also improved by that time, with at least some rudimentary suspension. The coach body was suspended on leather straps to absorb some of the road shock, but this caused the coach to sway constantly as it made its way over stony and rutted roads. This early form of public transport carried passengers for stages of ten or fifteen miles before the horses had to be changed.

Passengers could either sit inside the coach for the highest priced ticket, or on the outside, exposed to the elements, for a reduced fare. However much they paid, passengers were expected to get out and walk up steep hills to spare the horses and even to push the coach when its wheels became stuck in potholes. Highwaymen were a constant threat for all road users, so wealthy passengers began to wear paste jewellery, leaving their valuables at home whenever possible.

The coach would call at one of the many staging inns along the route. At the inn ostlers would change the team of horses while the passengers rested from hours of being swayed and jolted. They could either resume their journey as soon as the horses had been changed or stay overnight at the inn, continuing the journey the next morning with another coach.

Inns were noisy places, infamous for poor food and little comfort. Most inns had a cobbled courtyard for coaches to pull into, such as can still be seen at the Rose and Crown in Wisbech. The arrival of each coach clattering into the courtyard was announced with the sounding of a horn. This, with the noise of hooves on cobbles, the raised voices of coachmen and the passengers entering the inn, together with the inevitable slamming of doors at all hours of day and night, could hardly have been restful.

Other forms of public transport were the post-chaise and the mail coach. The post-chaise was a four-wheeled, yellow-coloured closed carriage, drawn by four horses. This was hired by the distance, with horses being changed at staging posts, as with stage coaches. The mail coach, as mentioned earlier, was principally to carry mail over a set route, though it could also carry passengers. It was known to be faster than the stage, because it only stopped for the delivery of mail, and not for the comfort of its passengers.

Roads finally began to improve, though very slowly, with the first turnpikes, which were established around 1750. At first, these were roads running through large estates that the landowner maintained in exchange for a fee at the turnpike. Gradually the number of these toll roads increased, improving many routes as well as the lot of the traveller. The first turnpike in the Wisbech area was opened in 1766 and ran from the ferry at Chatteris, via March and Wisbech, to Tydd Gote. A second turnpike was then built from Wisbech to Downham Market Bridge. The section of road from March to Wisbech ran for the last four miles into Wisbech along the top of the high Waldersea Bank and this soon became infamous. The road was surfaced with fine soil and was less than thirty feet wide. It was also perilously close to the river. It was so dangerous that most traffic refused to use it, except in full daylight and in perfect weather conditions. The situation was so bad that the mail from Guyhirn to Wisbech was sent by boat in winter, to avoid risking the road.

Roads elsewhere could be just as bad. The route from Norfolk to the Midlands, especially the section between Wisbech and Thorney, was notorious. Carts regularly became stuck fast in the mud and the road was considered impassible for six months of the year. Roads were not to improve until after 1810, when things finally began to change for the better.

Town streets were often as poor as the main routes and since the 1650s, the Sedan Chair had been a common sight in towns. Used by the better-off citizens, the Sedan was an enclosed small cabin carried by two men between two long poles. The single passenger entered the chair through a hinged doorway in the front, the roof being raised until he was seated. Many of the grander houses owned their own Sedan Chairs. They were extremely useful, as they could transport the passenger from door to door, and even through it, without him ever having to put a foot down onto the filthy street.

**Sedan Chair in the collection of Packwood House, National Trust.
Brackets for carrying poles can clearly be seen**

For greater distances, a gentleman had his horses and private carriage. Guiseppe Baretti in his letters about his stay in Wisbech mentions that the journey from London to Wisbech took him "a whole day and a short part of the night without stopping." However uncomfortable this would have been, it must have been a lot more convenient in his private carriage than in a stage coach.

Even when rain made roads impassible for a carriage, horses could be relied on for transport. One of the most popular breeds of horse for hunting, riding and for pulling a carriage was the Cleveland Bay, well loved for its bay colour, longevity, strength and quiet disposition. Larger households employed a groom to care for the horses and he would have travelled with the family on outings, to tend the horses on arrival. He rode on a small seat at the back of the carriage, where he was totally unprotected from the elements. Where the household was wealthy enough to support it, a coachman would be in charge of the stable boys and grooms and responsible for driving the coach. His driving seat was also unprotected from the weather, but he would have had some protection from his greatcoat; a thick coat with caped shoulders, which became standard dress for the post of coachman.

Inside the Georgian stables at Peckover House

A gentleman's carriage was as important an asset as a car is today and in the eighteenth century there were several popular types of conveyance.

A coach was a closed, four-wheeled vehicle pulled by between four and six horses. It had a fixed roof, doors and windows to protect the passengers. The coachman's seat was at the front, the groom's at the rear.

A curricle was a sporty two-wheeled, light weight carriage, drawn by two horses. This was the sports car of its time, a real must-have for the modern young gentleman about town.

The phaeton was also sporty, but had four wheels and was pulled by a single horse. This was intended to be driven by the owner himself and was able to negotiate sharp turns. The phaeton soon became well known as a vehicle for fast and often reckless driving. There was an opening roof, so that his passengers could enjoy fresh air as they rode along.

Life in the Georgian fast lane, so to speak, was a good one. Transport may have provided its frustrations, but town planning, farming and industry were beginning to shape the country we know today. Freedom of speech, still highly valued now, was encouraging debate and progress. More of the population was moving into towns and cities, their lives coloured, if only in some small part, by the cultural changes taking place around them. And Wisbech, however small, however marginalised in the Fenland of East Anglia, could not escape these influences.

Peckover House from the Croquet Lawn

Afterword

A Place in the Georgian World

It isn't known quite who built the townhouse on North Brink, but whether Cicely Lowe or one of the Stone brothers, it was commissioned in the latest style and made a bold statement about its residents' wealth and standing in the town.

And the town itself was booming. Despite the less than perfect river transport system, Wisbech throughout the eighteenth century was a busy, prosperous market town with a population that was to reach 4710 by the census of 1801. This same census also recorded that the number of inhabited houses in the town was 1008, which gives a good idea of the density of population at the time.

Wisbech had always been part of Fenland, its port and market vital for trade. The port was continuing a role that went back hundreds of years, as important to the medieval herdsman exporting his fleeces as to the Georgian farmer selling his flax seed for oil production. The effects of Enclosure were still being felt across Fenland, with whole rural communities struggling to adapt to losing their old way of life. The poverty and bitterness of the Fen Tigers was so profound that it can still be detected today.

Wisbech, however isolated it may have felt, was no back water. It was very much part of a rapidly developing world, as much at the mercy of political and social change as any other English town. Despite the many challenges it faced in keeping its river links alive, Wisbech was not only surviving, but growing, its port being at the heart of its expansion and prosperity.

Georgian Wisbech must have been a vibrant place. There

would have been almost constant activity on the quayside, with tall sailing ships bringing in goods from near and far. The constant noise and commotion, as imported goods were loaded onto lighters to be taken upstream or onto wagons to be moved by road, would have been central to town life. Added to this would be the weekly market traffic and noise; farmers and trades people bringing in their produce to sell, their voices crying out to advertise their wares to the town and country people who flocked in to buy. There would also be continuous activity around the inns, with the clatter of the mail coaches arriving and departing, bringing more visitors to the town.

As well as the noise, there were the smells. For much of the eighteenth century there were open sewers running down the centres of town streets, where all manner of rubbish would end up. As well as the street smells, personal hygiene was not given the priority it is today, so the general pong of the town with its relatively dense population, must have been noticed by visitors from the countryside, who were used to fresher air. Perhaps the general buzz of the place helped to make up for it. Servants running errands, bustling inns, ships on the quayside, market stalls and citizens of all ranks would have brought colour and variety to the muddy wide streets and narrow alleyways. With its grand houses, inns, market, its races, balls, suppers and theatre, Georgian Wisbech was certainly not a dull town. It was home to all classes, from seamstresses, scullery maids and farm labourers to merchants, burgesses, and land owners.

It was home too, to the residents of the house that was to become Peckover; to the Lakes, Marshalls, Southwells, the early Peckovers and to its many tenants and servants. It was built at a time of prosperity and was to endure through leaner times, years when Wisbech's early vitality would be all but forgotten.

But life, for all its progress and necessary change, can sometimes appear to move more in cycles than in straight lines. Peckover House is now safe in the care of the National Trust and attracts around 23,000 visitors a year. Its past is nurtured, while being a part of the present community, and its future is assured. And Wisbech too seems to be entering a new era, reawakening after too long of accepting a backwater status. At the beginning of a new century its port has been redeveloped and new shops and businesses are coming to town. It will perhaps never return to its Georgian heyday, but it can prosper again as a Fenland town, while honouring its long and intriguing history.

Thank You....

This may seem a very short book, but it has taken a great deal of research and to do that I've had to rely on the help of many local people. I am very grateful for their time, energy and willingness to help; this little history couldn't have been completed without them. They are (in the usual alphabetical order):

Robert Bell of Wisbech and Fenland Museum

Nigel Elgood of Elgood's Brewery

Michelle Lawes of Wisbech Castle

National Trust Photo Library (All photographs of items in their collections are reproduced with their kind permission.)

Roger Powell of the Wisbech Society

Ben Rickett of National Trust's Peckover House

Rose and Crown, Wisbech

Pat Sims, for her help with research at the exhibition stage

Spalding Gentlemen's Society

Rob Williams of Angles Theatre

Thanks also to my wonderful family; to Janet Calton, my mother, and Anthony Smith, my husband, for all their encouragement and for Tony's drawings, maps and long hours of proof reading. And not forgetting Linda Bedford for that first idea, or Mary Rawlings and Miss W Glavis for inspiration so many years ago.

Bibliography

Nancy Bradfield, "Historical Costumes of England 1066-1968"

Ingrid Cranfield, "Georgian House Style"

Daniel Defoe, "A Tour Through the Whole Island of Great Britain"

William Elstobb, "Plan of Wisbech Adjoining the River"

Henrietta Heald, (Editor) "The Chronicle of Britain and Ireland"

Peter Hewitt, "Fenland; A Landscape Made by Man"

Samuel Pepys' Diary

William Watson, "An Historical Account of the Ancient Town and Port of Wisbech"

John Wood, "Plan of Wisbech 1830."

James Woodforde, "The Diary of a Country Parson"